MznLnx

Missing Links Exam Preps

Exam Prep for

Calculus for Biology and Medicine
Neuhauser, 2nd Edition

The MznLnx Exam Prep is your link from the texbook and lecture to your exams.
The MznLnx Exam Preps are unauthorized and comprehensive reviews of your textbooks.

All material provided by MznLnx and Rico Publications (c) 2010
Textbook publishers and textbook authors do not particpate in or contribute to these reviews.

MznLnx

Rico Publications

Exam Prep for Calculus for Biology and Medicine
2nd Edition
Neuhauser

Publisher: Raymond Houge
Assistant Editor: Michael Rouger
Text and Cover Designer: Lisa Buckner
Marketing Manager: Sara Swagger
Project Manager, Editorial Production: Jerry Emerson
Art Director: Vernon Lowerui

Product Manager: Dave Mason
Editorial Assitant: Rachel Guzmanji
Pedagogy: Debra Long
Cover Image: Jim Reed/Getty Images
Text and Cover Printer: City Printing, Inc.
Compositor: Media Mix, Inc.

(c) 2010 Rico Publications
ALL RIGHTS RESERVED. No part of this work covered by the copyright may be reproduced or used in any form or by an means--graphic, electronic, or mechanical, including photocopying, recording, taping, Web distribution, information storage, and retrieval systems, or in any other manner--without the written permission of the publisher.

For more information about our products, contact us at:
Dave.Mason@RicoPublications.com

For permission to use material from this text or product, submit a request online to:
Dave.Mason@RicoPublications.com

Printed in the United States
ISBN:

Contents

CHAPTER 1
PREVIEW AND REVIEW 1

CHAPTER 2
DISCRETE TIME MODELS, SEQUENCES, AND DIFFERENCE EQUATIONS 23

CHAPTER 3
LIMITS AND CONTINUITY 31

CHAPTER 4
DIFFERENTIATION 42

CHAPTER 5
APPLICATIONS OF DIFFERENTIATION 58

CHAPTER 6
INTEGRATION 74

CHAPTER 7
INTEGRATION TECHNIQUES AND COMPUTATIONAL METHODS 87

CHAPTER 8
DIFFERENTIAL EQUATIONS 97

CHAPTER 9
LINEAR ALGEBRA AND ANALYTIC GEOMETRY 107

CHAPTER 10
MULTIVARIABLE CALCULUS 118

CHAPTER 11
SYSTEMS OF DIFFFRENTIAL EQUATIONS 122

CHAPTER 12
PROBABILITY AND STATISTICS 125

ANSWER KEY 136

TO THE STUDENT

COMPREHENSIVE

The *MznLnx* Exam Prep series is designed to help you pass your exams. Editors at MznLnx review your textbooks and then prepare these practice exams to help you master the textbook material. Unlike study guides, workbooks, and practice tests provided by the texbook publisher and textbook authors, *MznLnx* gives you **all** of the material in each chapter in exam form, not just samples, so you can be sure to nail your exam.

MECHANICAL

The MznLnx Exam Prep series creates exams that will help you learn the subject matter as well as test you on your understanding. Each question is designed to help you master the concept. Just working through the exams, you gain an understanding of the subject--its a simple mechanical process that produces success.

INTEGRATED STUDY GUIDE AND REVIEW

MznLnx is not just a set of exams designed to test you, its also a comprehensive review of the subject content. Each exam question is also a review of the concept, making sure that you will get the answer correct without having to go to other sources of material. You learn as you go! Its the easiest way to pass an exam.

HUMOR

Studying can be tedious and dry. MznLnx's instructional design includes moderate humor within the exam questions on occassion, to break the tedium and revitalize the brain

Chapter 1. PREVIEW AND REVIEW

1. The _____ of a function is an extension of the concept of a sum, and are identified or found through the use of integration.
   a. Integral0
   b. Thing
   c. Undefined
   d. Undefined

2. _____ is a mathematical subject that includes the study of limits, derivatives, integrals, and power series and constitutes a major part of modern university curriculum.
   a. Calculus0
   b. Thing
   c. Undefined
   d. Undefined

3. A _____ is traditionally an infinitesimally small change in a variable.
   a. Thing
   b. Differential0
   c. Undefined
   d. Undefined

4. In trigonometry, the _____ is a function defined as $\tan x = {\sin x}/{\cos x}$. The function is so-named because it can be defined as the length of a certain segment of a _____ (in the geometric sense) to the unit circle. In plane geometry, a line is _____ to a curve, at some point, if both line and curve pass through the point with the same direction.
   a. Thing
   b. Tangent0
   c. Undefined
   d. Undefined

5. _____ has two distinct but etymologically-related meanings: one in geometry and one in trigonometry.
   a. Tangent line0
   b. Thing
   c. Undefined
   d. Undefined

6. In mathematics, the concept of a _____ tries to capture the intuitive idea of a geometrical one-dimensional and continuous object. A simple example is the circle.
   a. Thing
   b. Curve0
   c. Undefined
   d. Undefined

7. In mathematics, _____ are the intuitive idea of a geometrical one-dimensional and continuous object.
   a. Curves0
   b. Thing
   c. Undefined
   d. Undefined

8. in mathematics, maxima and minima, known collectively as _____, are the largest value maximum or smallest value minimum, that a function takes in a point either within a given neighborhood or on the function domain in its entirety global extremum.
   a. Extrema0
   b. Thing
   c. Undefined
   d. Undefined

9. _____ is a free computer algebra system based on a 1982 version of Macsyma
   a. Maxima0
   b. Thing
   c. Undefined
   d. Undefined

10. _____ are points in the domain of a function at which the function takes a largest value or smallest value, either within a given neighborhood or on the function domain in its entirety.

Chapter 1. PREVIEW AND REVIEW

    a. Thing
    b. Maxima and minima0
    c. Undefined
    d. Undefined

11. _____, a field in mathematics, is the study of how functions change when their inputs change. The primary object of study in _____ is the derivative.
    a. Thing
    b. Differential calculus0
    c. Undefined
    d. Undefined

12. In mathematics, maxima and _____, known collectively as extrema, are points in the domain of a function at which the function takes a largest value.
    a. Thing
    b. Minima0
    c. Undefined
    d. Undefined

13. The _____ of a solid object is the three-dimensional concept of how much space it occupies, often quantified numerically.
    a. Thing
    b. Volume0
    c. Undefined
    d. Undefined

14. In mathematics, _____ geometry was the traditional name for the geometry of three-dimensional Euclidean space — for practical purposes the kind of space we live in.
    a. Solid0
    b. Thing
    c. Undefined
    d. Undefined

15. In mathematics, a _____ of a complex-valued function f is a member x of the domain of f such that f(x) vanishes at x, that is, x : f (x) = 0.
    a. Thing
    b. Root0
    c. Undefined
    d. Undefined

16. In mathematical analysis and related areas of mathematics, a set is called _____, if it is, in a certain sense, of finite size.
    a. Bounded0
    b. Thing
    c. Undefined
    d. Undefined

17. _____ element of an element x with respect to a binary operation * with identity element e is an element y such that x * y = y * x = e. In particular,
    a. Thing
    b. Inverse0
    c. Undefined
    d. Undefined

18. In mathematics, the _____ of a function is the set of all "output" values produced by that function. Given a function $f : A \to B$, the _____ of f, is defined to be the set $\{x \in B : x = f(a) \text{ for some } a \in A\}$.
    a. Thing
    b. Range0
    c. Undefined
    d. Undefined

19. In mathematics, a _____ is a countable collection of open covers of a topological space that satisfies certain separation axioms.

Chapter 1. PREVIEW AND REVIEW

    a. Thing
    b. Development0
    c. Undefined
    d. Undefined

20. _____ is often used to describe the measurement of the steepness, incline, gradient, or grade of a straight line. The _____ is defined as the ratio of the "rise" divided by the "run" between two points on a line, or in other words, the ratio of the altitude change to the horizontal distance between any two points on the line.
    a. Slope0
    b. Thing
    c. Undefined
    d. Undefined

21. The mathematical concept of a _____ expresses the intuitive idea of deterministic dependence between two quantities, one of which is viewed as primary and the other as secondary. A _____ then is a way to associate a unique output for each input of a specified type, for example, a real number or an element of a given set.
    a. Function0
    b. Thing
    c. Undefined
    d. Undefined

22. A _____ is a special kind of ratio, indicating a relationship between two measurements with different units, such as miles to gallons or cents to pounds.
    a. Thing
    b. Rate0
    c. Undefined
    d. Undefined

23. In sociology and biology a _____ is the collection of people or organisms of a particular species living in a given geographic area or space, usually measured by a census.
    a. Population0
    b. Thing
    c. Undefined
    d. Undefined

24. _____ is change in population over time, and can be quantified as the change in the number of individuals in a population per unit time.
    a. Population growth0
    b. Thing
    c. Undefined
    d. Undefined

25. Deductive _____ is the kind of _____ in which the conclusion is necessitated by, or reached from, previously known facts (the premises).
    a. Reasoning0
    b. Thing
    c. Undefined
    d. Undefined

26. A _____ is a one-dimensional picture in which the integers are shown as specially-marked points evenly spaced on a line.
    a. Thing
    b. Number line0
    c. Undefined
    d. Undefined

27. In mathematics, a _____ may be described informally as a number that can be given by an infinite decimal representation.
    a. Thing
    b. Real number0
    c. Undefined
    d. Undefined

Chapter 1. PREVIEW AND REVIEW

28. In elementary algebra, an _____ is a set that contains every real number between two indicated numbers and may contain the two numbers themselves.
    - a. Thing
    - b. Interval0
    - c. Undefined
    - d. Undefined

29. Mathematical _____ is used to represent ideas.
    - a. Notation0
    - b. Thing
    - c. Undefined
    - d. Undefined

30. In mathematics, the _____ of a coordinate system is the point where the axes of the system intersect.
    - a. Thing
    - b. Origin0
    - c. Undefined
    - d. Undefined

31. In mathematics, the _____ (or modulus) of a real number is its numerical value without regard to its sign.
    - a. Absolute value0
    - b. Thing
    - c. Undefined
    - d. Undefined

32. Equivalence is the condition of being _____ or essentially equal.
    - a. Thing
    - b. Equivalent0
    - c. Undefined
    - d. Undefined

33. The word _____ comes from the Latin word linearis, which means created by lines.
    - a. Thing
    - b. Linear0
    - c. Undefined
    - d. Undefined

34. A _____ is an equation in which each term is either a constant or the product of a constant times the first power of a variable.
    - a. Linear equation0
    - b. Thing
    - c. Undefined
    - d. Undefined

35. A _____ is a symbolic representation denoting a quantity or expression. It often represents an "unknown" quantity that has the potential to change.
    - a. Thing
    - b. Variable0
    - c. Undefined
    - d. Undefined

36. _____ is a notation for writing numbers that is often used by scientists and mathematicians to make it easier to write large and small numbers.
    - a. Thing
    - b. Scientific notation0
    - c. Undefined
    - d. Undefined

37. In mathematics and the mathematical sciences, a _____ is a fixed, but possibly unspecified, value. This is in contrast to a variable, which is not fixed.
    - a. Thing
    - b. Constant0
    - c. Undefined
    - d. Undefined

38. _____ is a branch of mathematics concerning the study of structure, relation and quantity.

a. Concept
b. Algebra0
c. Undefined
d. Undefined

39. In mathematics, two quantities are called _____ if they vary in such a way that one of the quantities is a constant multiple of the other, or equivalently if they have a constant ratio.
   a. Proportional0
   b. Thing
   c. Undefined
   d. Undefined

40. _____ is a special mathematical relationship between two quantities. Two quantities are called proportional if they vary in such a way that one of the quantities is a constant multiple of the other, or equivalently if they have a constant ratio.
   a. Thing
   b. Proportionality0
   c. Undefined
   d. Undefined

41. In geometry, the _____ of an object is a point in some sense in the middle of the object.
   a. Thing
   b. Center0
   c. Undefined
   d. Undefined

42. In Euclidean geometry, a _____ is the set of all points in a plane at a fixed distance, called the radius, from a given point, the center.
   a. Circle0
   b. Thing
   c. Undefined
   d. Undefined

43. In classical geometry, a _____ of a circle or sphere is any line segment from its center to its boundary. By extension, the _____ of a circle or sphere is the length of any such segment. The _____ is half the diameter. In science and engineering the term _____ of curvature is commonly used as a synonym for _____.
   a. Thing
   b. Radius0
   c. Undefined
   d. Undefined

44. _____ is a relation in Euclidean geometry among the three sides of a right triangle.
   a. Pythagorean Theorem0
   b. Thing
   c. Undefined
   d. Undefined

45. _____ is a circle with a unit radius, i.e., a circle whose radius is 1.
   a. Unit circle0
   b. Thing
   c. Undefined
   d. Undefined

46. In mathematics, a _____ is a statement that can be proved on the basis of explicitly stated or previously agreed assumptions.
   a. Theorem0
   b. Thing
   c. Undefined
   d. Undefined

47. _____ is a branch of mathematics which deals with triangles, particularly triangles in a plane where one angle of the triangle is 90 degrees, and a variety of other topological relations such as spheres, in other branches, such as spherical _____.

Chapter 1. PREVIEW AND REVIEW

   a. Thing
   b. Trigonometry0
   c. Undefined
   d. Undefined

48. In mathematics, a _____ is a two-dimensional manifold or surface that is perfectly flat.
   a. Plane0
   b. Thing
   c. Undefined
   d. Undefined

49. The _____ is a unit of plane angle. It is represented by the symbol "rad" or, more rarely, by the superscript c (for "circular measure"). For example, an angle of 1.2 radians would be written "1.2 rad" or "1.2c" (second symbol can produce confusion with centigrads).
   a. Thing
   b. Radian0
   c. Undefined
   d. Undefined

50. In mathematics, there are several meanings of _____ depending on the subject.
   a. Thing
   b. Degree0
   c. Undefined
   d. Undefined

51. In mathematics, the _____ functions are functions of an angle; they are important when studying triangles and modeling periodic phenomena, among many other applications.
   a. Thing
   b. Trigonometric0
   c. Undefined
   d. Undefined

52. The _____ are functions of an angle; they are important when studying triangles and modeling periodic phenomena, among many other applications.
   a. Trigonometric functions0
   b. Thing
   c. Undefined
   d. Undefined

53. _____ is a trigonemtric function that is important when studying triangles and modeling periodic phenomena, among other applications.
   a. Sine0
   b. Thing
   c. Undefined
   d. Undefined

54. _____ is a term in Trigonometry used to describe the secant of the complement of a cirlce.
   a. Thing
   b. Cosecant0
   c. Undefined
   d. Undefined

55. The _____ of an angle is the ratio of the length of the adjacent side to the length of the hypotenuse.
   a. Cosine0
   b. Concept
   c. Undefined
   d. Undefined

56. _____ is the ratio of the adjacent to the opposite side of a right-angeled triangle
   a. Cotangent0
   b. Thing
   c. Undefined
   d. Undefined

57. _____ is a unit of plane angle, equal to 180/δ degrees, or about 57.2958 degrees

Chapter 1. PREVIEW AND REVIEW

    a. Radian measure0   b. Thing
    c. Undefined   d. Undefined

58. A _____ is a function that assigns a number to subsets of a given set.
    a. Thing   b. Measure0
    c. Undefined   d. Undefined

59. _____ is a trigonometric function that is the reciprocal of cosine.
    a. Secant0   b. Thing
    c. Undefined   d. Undefined

60. A _____ is one of the basic shapes of geometry: a polygon with three vertices and three sides which are straight line segments.
    a. Thing   b. Triangle0
    c. Undefined   d. Undefined

61. An _____ is an equality that remains true regardless of the values of any variables that appear within it, to distinguish it from an equality which is true under more particular conditions.
    a. Thing   b. Identity0
    c. Undefined   d. Undefined

62. In mathematics, _____ growth occurs when the growth rate of a function is always proportional to the function's current size.
    a. Thing   b. Exponential0
    c. Undefined   d. Undefined

63. In mathematics, a _____ of a number x is the exponent y of the power by such that $x = b^y$. The value used for the base b must be neither 0 nor 1, nor a root of 1 in the case of the extension to complex numbers, and is typically 10, e, or 2.
    a. Logarithm0   b. Thing
    c. Undefined   d. Undefined

64. An _____ is a combination of numbers, operators, grouping symbols and/or free variables and bound variables arranged in a meaningful way which can be evaluated..
    a. Expression0   b. Thing
    c. Undefined   d. Undefined

65. In mathematics, a _____ number is a number which can be expressed as a ratio of two integers. Non-integer _____ numbers (commonly called fractions) are usually written as the vulgar fraction a / b, where b is not zero.
    a. Thing   b. Rational0
    c. Undefined   d. Undefined

66. _____ is a mathematical operation, written a^n, involving two numbers, the base a and the exponent n.
    a. Thing   b. Exponentiating0
    c. Undefined   d. Undefined

67. _____ is a mathematical operation, written a^n, involving two numbers, the base a and the exponent n.

Chapter 1. PREVIEW AND REVIEW

a. Exponentiation0
b. Thing
c. Undefined
d. Undefined

68. _____ is the logarithm to the base e, where e is an irrational constant approximately equal to 2.718281828459.
   a. Natural logarithm0
   b. Thing
   c. Undefined
   d. Undefined

69. In mathematics, an _____ number is any real number that is not a rational number- that is, it is a number which cannot be expressed as a fraction m/n, where m and n are integers.
   a. Thing
   b. Irrational0
   c. Undefined
   d. Undefined

70. In mathematics, an _____ is any real number that is not a rational number ¡ª that is, it is a number which cannot be expressed as m/n, where m and n are integers.
   a. Thing
   b. Irrational number0
   c. Undefined
   d. Undefined

71. In mathematics, a _____ is a number in the form of a + bi where a and b are real numbers, and i is the imaginary unit, with the property $i^2 = -1$. The real number a is called the real part of the _____, and the real number b is the imaginary part.
   a. Thing
   b. Complex number0
   c. Undefined
   d. Undefined

72. In mathematics, the _____ of a complex number z, is the first element of the ordered pair of real numbers representing z, i.e. if z = (x,y), or equivalently, z = x + iy, then the _____ of z is x. It is denoted by Re{z}. The complex function which maps z to the _____ of z is not holomorphic.
   a. Thing
   b. Real part0
   c. Undefined
   d. Undefined

73. In mathematics, an _____ number is a complex number whose square is a negative real number. They were defined in 1572 by Rafael Bombelli.
   a. Imaginary0
   b. Thing
   c. Undefined
   d. Undefined

74. In mathematics, the _____ of a complex number z, is the second element of the ordered pair of real numbers representing z, i.e. if z = (x,y), or equivalently, z = x + iy, then the _____ of z is y.
   a. Imaginary part0
   b. Thing
   c. Undefined
   d. Undefined

75. In mathematics, an _____ is a complex number whose square is a negative real number. They were defined in 1572 by Rafael Bombelli.
   a. Imaginary number0
   b. Thing
   c. Undefined
   d. Undefined

76. In mathematics, a _____ is the result of multiplying, or an expression that identifies factors to be multiplied.

Chapter 1. PREVIEW AND REVIEW

a. Thing
b. Product0
c. Undefined
d. Undefined

77. The _____ relates to the binary operation of multiplication and addition.
   a. Thing
   b. Distributive law0
   c. Undefined
   d. Undefined

78. In algebra, a _____ is a binomial formed by taking the opposite of the second term of a binomial.
   a. Thing
   b. Conjugate0
   c. Undefined
   d. Undefined

79. In mathematics, a _____ is a polynomial equation of the second degree. The general form is $ax^2 + bx + c = 0$.
   a. Thing
   b. Quadratic equation0
   c. Undefined
   d. Undefined

80. A quadratic equation with real solutions, called roots, which may be real or complex, is given by the _____: $x = \frac{-b \pm \sqrt{b^2 - 4ac}}{2a}$.
   a. Thing
   b. Quadratic formula0
   c. Undefined
   d. Undefined

81. _____ is a set of numbers, in the broadest sense of the word, together with one or more operations, such as addition or multiplication.
   a. Number system0
   b. Thing
   c. Undefined
   d. Undefined

82. The _____ integers are all the integers from zero on upwards.
   a. Nonnegative0
   b. Thing
   c. Undefined
   d. Undefined

83. _____ of a polynomial with real or complex coefficients is a certain expression in the coefficients of the polynomial which is equal to zero if and only if the polynomial has a multiple root i.e. a root with multiplicity greater than one in the complex numbers.
   a. Discriminant0
   b. Thing
   c. Undefined
   d. Undefined

84. In astronomy, geography, geometry and related sciences and contexts, a plane is said to be _____ at a given point if it is locally perpendicular to the gradient of the gravity field, i.e., with the direction of the gravitational force at that point.
   a. Thing
   b. Horizontal0
   c. Undefined
   d. Undefined

85. In geometry, two lines or planes if one falls on the other in such a way as to create congruent adjacent angles. The term may be used as a noun or adjective. Thus, referring to Figure 1, the line AB is the _____ to CD through the point B.
   a. Thing
   b. Perpendicular0
   c. Undefined
   d. Undefined

Chapter 1. PREVIEW AND REVIEW

86. The _____ or kilogramme is the SI base unit of mass. It is defined as being equal to the mass of the international prototype of the _____.
 a. Thing
 b. Kilogram0
 c. Undefined
 d. Undefined

87. _____ is the transport of people on a trip/journey or the process or time involved in a person or object moving from one location to another.
 a. Thing
 b. Travel0
 c. Undefined
 d. Undefined

88. In plane geometry, a _____ is a polygon with four equal sides, four right angles, and parallel opposite sides. In algebra, the _____ of a number is that number multiplied by itself.
 a. Thing
 b. Square0
 c. Undefined
 d. Undefined

89. A _____ (symbol ha) is a unit of area, equal to 10,000 square metres, commonly used for measuring land area. Its base unit, the are, was defined by older forms of the metric system, but neither it nor the _____ are part of the modern metric system.
 a. Concept
 b. Hectare0
 c. Undefined
 d. Undefined

90. The _____ of measurement are a globally standardized and modernized form of the metric system.
 a. Units0
 b. Thing
 c. Undefined
 d. Undefined

91. _____ is the estimation of a physical quantity such as distance, energy, temperature, or time.
 a. Thing
 b. Measurement0
 c. Undefined
 d. Undefined

92. A _____ is a unit of length in the metric system, equal to one thousand metres, the current SI base unit of length
 a. Thing
 b. Kilometer0
 c. Undefined
 d. Undefined

93. A _____ is a unit of length, usually used to measure distance, in a number of different systems, including Imperial units, United States customary units and Norwegian/Swedish mil. Its size can vary from system to system, but in each is between 1 and 10 kilometers. In contemporary English contexts _____ refers to either:
 a. Mile0
 b. Thing
 c. Undefined
 d. Undefined

94. _____ is a unit of speed, expressing the number of international miles covered per hour.
 a. Thing
 b. Miles per hour0
 c. Undefined
 d. Undefined

95. _____ is a temperature scale named after the German physicist Daniel Gabriel _____ , who proposed it in 1724.

Chapter 1. PREVIEW AND REVIEW

a. Fahrenheit0
b. Thing
c. Undefined
d. Undefined

96. _____ is, or relates to, the _____ temperature scale .
   a. Celsius0
   b. Thing
   c. Undefined
   d. Undefined

97. _____ is a physical property of a system that underlies the common notions of hot and cold; something that is hotter has the greater _____.
   a. Thing
   b. Temperature0
   c. Undefined
   d. Undefined

98. In Euclidean geometry, a uniform _____ is a linear transformation that enlargers or diminishes objects, and whose _____ factor is the same in all directions. This is also called homothethy.
   a. Thing
   b. Scale0
   c. Undefined
   d. Undefined

99. Celsius is, or relates to, the Celsius temperature scale (previously known as the centigrade scale). The degree Celsius (symbol: °C) can refer to a specific temperature on the _____ as well as serve as unit increment to indicate a temperature interval (a difference between two temperatures or an uncertainty).
   a. Celsius Scale0
   b. Concept
   c. Undefined
   d. Undefined

100. An _____ is a straight line around which a geometric figure can be rotated.
   a. Thing
   b. Axis0
   c. Undefined
   d. Undefined

101. An _____ Is when two lInes Intersect somewhere on a plane creating a right angle at Intersection
   a. Thing
   b. Axes0
   c. Undefined
   d. Undefined

102. _____ is electromagnetic radiation with a wavelength that is visible to the eye (visible _____) or, in a technical or scientific context, electromagnetic radiation of any wavelength.
   a. Light0
   b. Thing
   c. Undefined
   d. Undefined

103. In mathematics, a _____ is an algebraic structure in which addition and multiplication are defined and have properties listed below.
   a. Thing
   b. Ring0
   c. Undefined
   d. Undefined

104. _____ is a kind of property which exists as magnitude or multitude. It is among the basic classes of things along with quality, substance, change, and relation.
   a. Amount0
   b. Thing
   c. Undefined
   d. Undefined

105. _____ is mass m per unit volume V.
 a. Density0
 b. Thing
 c. Undefined
 d. Undefined

106. _____ was a German mathematician and philosopher. He invented calculus independently of Newton, and his notation is the one in general use since.
 a. Person
 b. Leibniz0
 c. Undefined
 d. Undefined

107. The _____, the average in everyday English, which is also called the arithmetic _____ (and is distinguished from the geometric _____ or harmonic _____). The average is also called the sample _____. The expected value of a random variable, which is also called the population _____.
 a. Thing
 b. Mean0
 c. Undefined
 d. Undefined

108. An _____ or member of a set is an object that when collected together make up the set.
 a. Thing
 b. Element0
 c. Undefined
 d. Undefined

109. A _____ is a set whose members are members of another set or a set contained within another set.
 a. Thing
 b. Subset0
 c. Undefined
 d. Undefined

110. _____ are groups whose members are members of another set or a set contained within another set.
 a. Thing
 b. Subsets0
 c. Undefined
 d. Undefined

111. In mathematics, the _____ of a function f : X → Y is the set Y.
 a. Thing
 b. Codomain0
 c. Undefined
 d. Undefined

112. In mathematics, _____ is a part of the set theoretic notion of function.
 a. Image0
 b. Thing
 c. Undefined
 d. Undefined

113. In mathematics, a _____ of a k-place relation $L \subseteq X_1 \times ... \times X_k$ is one of the sets X_j, $1 \leq j \leq k$. In the special case where k = 2 and $L \subseteq X_1 \times X_2$ is a function $L : X_1 \to X_2$, it is conventional to refer to X_1 as the _____ of the function and to refer to X_2 as the codomain of the function.
 a. Thing
 b. Domain0
 c. Undefined
 d. Undefined

114. In mathematics, an _____ is any of the arguments, i.e. "inputs", to a function. Thus if we have a function f(x), then x is a _____.
 a. Thing
 b. Independent variable0
 c. Undefined
 d. Undefined

Chapter 1. PREVIEW AND REVIEW

115. In a function the _____, is the variable which is the value, i.e. the "output", of the function.
 a. Dependent variable0
 b. Thing
 c. Undefined
 d. Undefined

116. A _____ number is a positive integer which has a positive divisor other than one or itself.
 a. Thing
 b. Composite0
 c. Undefined
 d. Undefined

117. A _____, formed by the composition of one function on another, represents the application of the former to the result of the application of the latter to the argument of the composite.
 a. Thing
 b. Composite function0
 c. Undefined
 d. Undefined

118. In mathematics, a _____ of a positive integer n is a way of writing n as a sum of positive integers.
 a. Thing
 b. Composition0
 c. Undefined
 d. Undefined

119. In mathematics, a _____ is an expression that is constructed from one or more variables and constants, using only the operations of addition, subtraction, multiplication, and constant positive whole number exponents. is a _____. Note in particular that division by an expression containing a variable is not in general allowed in polynomials. [1]
 a. Polynomial0
 b. Thing
 c. Undefined
 d. Undefined

120. In mathematics, a _____ is a constant multiplicative factor of a certain object. The object can be such things as a variable, a vector, a function, etc. For example, the _____ of $9x^2$ is 9.
 a. Coefficient0
 b. Thing
 c. Undefined
 d. Undefined

121. _____ is the property of a physical object that quantifies the amount of matter and energy it is equivalent to.
 a. Thing
 b. Mass0
 c. Undefined
 d. Undefined

122. In mathematics, a _____ is any function which can be written as the ratio of two polynomial functions.
 a. Thing
 b. Rational function0
 c. Undefined
 d. Undefined

123. _____ of an object is its speed in a particular direction.
 a. Velocity0
 b. Thing
 c. Undefined
 d. Undefined

124. In mathematics, a _____ is a type of conic section defined as the intersection between a right circular conical surface and a plane which cuts through both halves of the cone.
 a. Thing
 b. Hyperbola0
 c. Undefined
 d. Undefined

125. _____ has many meanings, most of which simply .

a. Thing
b. Power0
c. Undefined
d. Undefined

126. _____ is a synonym for information.
a. Thing
b. Data0
c. Undefined
d. Undefined

127. A _____ is a three-dimensional solid object bounded by six square faces, facets, or sides, with three meeting at each vertex.
a. Cube0
b. Thing
c. Undefined
d. Undefined

128. _____ is one of the most important functions in mathematics. A function commonly used to study growth and decay
a. Exponential function0
b. Thing
c. Undefined
d. Undefined

129. In mathematics, _____ occurs when the growth rate of a function is always proportional to the function's current size.
a. Thing
b. Exponential growth0
c. Undefined
d. Undefined

130. A _____ is a negotiable instrument instructing a financial institution to pay a specific amount of a specific currency from a specific demand account held in the maker/depositor's name with that institution. Both the maker and payee may be natural persons or legal entities.
a. Thing
b. Check0
c. Undefined
d. Undefined

131. Initial objects are also called _____, and terminal objects are also called final.
a. Coterminal0
b. Thing
c. Undefined
d. Undefined

132. _____ is the process in which an unstable atomic nucleus loses energy by emitting radiation in the form of particles or electromagnetic waves.
a. Thing
b. Radioactive decay0
c. Undefined
d. Undefined

133. In linear algebra, the _____ of an n-by-n square matrix A is defined to be the sum of the elements on the main diagonal of A,
a. Thing
b. Trace0
c. Undefined
d. Undefined

134. A _____ is a quantity that denotes the proportional amount or magnitude of one quantity relative to another.
a. Thing
b. Ratio0
c. Undefined
d. Undefined

Chapter 1. PREVIEW AND REVIEW

135. In economics, economic _____ is simply a state of the world where economic forces are balanced and in the absence of external influences the values of economic variables will not change.
 a. Thing
 b. Equilibrium0
 c. Undefined
 d. Undefined

136. In business, particularly accounting, a _____ is the time intervals that the accounts, statement, payments, or other calculations cover.
 a. Period0
 b. Thing
 c. Undefined
 d. Undefined

137. A _____ is a numeral used to indicate a count. The most common use of the word today is to name the part of a fraction that tells the number or count of equal parts.
 a. Thing
 b. Numerator0
 c. Undefined
 d. Undefined

138. A _____ is the part of a fraction that tells how many equal parts make up a whole, and which is used in the name of the fraction: "halves", "thirds", "fourths" or "quarters", "fifths" and so on.
 a. Denominator0
 b. Concept
 c. Undefined
 d. Undefined

139. An _____ is a function which does the reverse of a given function.
 a. Inverse function0
 b. Thing
 c. Undefined
 d. Undefined

140. _____ is a test used to determine if a function is injective, surjective or bijective.
 a. Thing
 b. Horizontal line test0
 c. Undefined
 d. Undefined

141. Acid _____ ratio measures the ability of a company to use its near cash or quick assets to immediately extinguish its current liabilities.
 a. Thing
 b. Test0
 c. Undefined
 d. Undefined

142. _____ are the basic objects of study in graph theory. Informally speaking, a graph is a set of objects called points, nodes, or vertices connected by links called lines or edges.
 a. Graphs0
 b. Thing
 c. Undefined
 d. Undefined

143. In mathematics, a _____ (also spelled reflexion) is a map that transforms an object into its mirror image.
 a. Reflection0
 b. Concept
 c. Undefined
 d. Undefined

144. If the probabilities of simple events are all the same, then they are _____. This occurs in a uniform sample space.

Chapter 1. PREVIEW AND REVIEW

a. Equally likely0
b. Thing
c. Undefined
d. Undefined

145. In mathematics, a _____ is an ordered list of objects. Like a set, it contains members, also called elements or terms, and the number of terms is called the length of the _____. Unlike a set, order matters, and the exact same elements can appear multiple times at different positions in the _____.
a. Sequence0
b. Thing
c. Undefined
d. Undefined

146. _____ is an operator that measures the magnitude of a vector field's source or sink at a given point; the _____ of a vector field is a signed scalar.
a. Thing
b. Divergence0
c. Undefined
d. Undefined

147. A _____ is an abstract model that uses mathematical language to describe the behavior of a system. Eykhoff defined a _____ as 'a representation of the essential aspects of an existing system which presents knowledge of that system in usable form'.
a. Mathematical model0
b. Thing
c. Undefined
d. Undefined

148. A _____ of a number is the product of that number with any integer.
a. Thing
b. Multiple0
c. Undefined
d. Undefined

149. The _____ is a nonnegative scalar measure of a wave's magnitude of oscillation, that is, the magnitude of the maximum disturbance in the medium during one wave cycle.
a. Amplitude0
b. Thing
c. Undefined
d. Undefined

150. In mathematics, a _____ number is a real or complex number which is not algebraic, that is, not a solution of a non-zero polynomial equation, with rational coefficients.
a. Transcendental0
b. Thing
c. Undefined
d. Undefined

151. _____ means "constancy", i.e. if something retains a certain feature even after we change a way of looking at it, then it is symmetric.
a. Symmetry0
b. Thing
c. Undefined
d. Undefined

152. A _____ is a set of numbers that designate location in a given reference system, such as x,y in a planar _____ system or an x,y,z in a three-dimensional _____ system.
a. Coordinate0
b. Thing
c. Undefined
d. Undefined

153. In mathematics and its applications, a _____ is a system for assigning an n-tuple of numbers or scalars to each point in an n-dimensional space.

a. Coordinate system
b. Concept
c. Undefined
d. Undefined

154. _____ are functions which satisfy particular symmetry relations, with respect to taking additive inverses.
   a. Even function
   b. Thing
   c. Undefined
   d. Undefined

155. The _____ are the only integral domain whose positive elements are well-ordered, and in which order is preserved by addition. Like the natural numbers, the _____ form a countably infinite set. The set of all _____ is usually denoted in mathematics by a boldface Z .
   a. Integers
   b. Thing
   c. Undefined
   d. Undefined

156. _____ is a subset of a population.
   a. Sample
   b. Thing
   c. Undefined
   d. Undefined

157. _____ was an Austrian-born biologist known as one of the founders of general systems theory.
   a. Von Bertalanffy
   b. Person
   c. Undefined
   d. Undefined

158. In mathematics, the multiplicative inverse of a number x, denoted 1/x or x^{-1}, is the number which, when multiplied by x, yields 1. The multiplicative inverse of x is also called the _____ of x.
   a. Reciprocal
   b. Thing
   c. Undefined
   d. Undefined

159. The word _____ is used in a variety of ways in mathematics.
   a. Thing
   b. Index
   c. Undefined
   d. Undefined

160. In mathematics, a _____ in elementary terms is any of a variety of different functions from geometry, such as rotations, reflections and translations.
   a. Thing
   b. Transformation
   c. Undefined
   d. Undefined

161. In Euclidean geometry, a _____ is moving every point a constant distance in a specified direction.
   a. Concept
   b. Translation
   c. Undefined
   d. Undefined

162. In mathematics a _____ is a function which defines a distance between elements of a set.
   a. Metric
   b. Thing
   c. Undefined
   d. Undefined

163. _____ is a unit of length in the metric system, equal to one billionth of a metre, which is the current SI base unit of length.

Chapter 1. PREVIEW AND REVIEW

a. Thing
b. Nanometer0
c. Undefined
d. Undefined

164. The metre (or _____, see spelling differences) is a measure of length. It is the basic unit of length in the metric system and in the International System of Units (SI), used around the world for general and scientific purposes.
    a. Meter0
    b. Concept
    c. Undefined
    d. Undefined

165. A _____ is a first degree polynomial mathematical function of the form: $f(x) = mx + b$ where m and b are real constants and x is a real variable.
    a. Linear function0
    b. Thing
    c. Undefined
    d. Undefined

166. One of the three formats applicable to a quadratic function is the _____ which is defined as $f = ax^2 + bx + c$.
    a. General form0
    b. Thing
    c. Undefined
    d. Undefined

167. The _____ of a mathematical object is its size: a property by which it can be larger or smaller than other objects of the same kind; in technical terms, an ordering of the class of objects to which it belongs.
    a. Magnitude0
    b. Thing
    c. Undefined
    d. Undefined

168. A _____ consists of one quarter of the coordinate plane.
    a. Thing
    b. Quadrant0
    c. Undefined
    d. Undefined

169. In geographic information systems, a _____ comprises an entity with a geographic location, typically determined by points, arcs, or polygons. Carriageways and cadastres exemplify _____ data.
    a. Feature0
    b. Thing
    c. Undefined
    d. Undefined

170. In mathematics, the term _____ is applied to certain functions. There are two common ways it is applied: these are related historically, but diverged somewhat during the twentieth century.
    a. Functional0
    b. Thing
    c. Undefined
    d. Undefined

171. In mathematics, a set is called _____ if there is a bijection between the set and some set of the form {1, 2, ..., n} where n is a natural number.
    a. Thing
    b. Finite0
    c. Undefined
    d. Undefined

172. _____ is a set, with some particular properties and usually some additional structure, such as the operations of addition or multiplication, for instance.
    a. Space0
    b. Thing
    c. Undefined
    d. Undefined

Chapter 1. PREVIEW AND REVIEW

173. In geometry, a _____ (Greek words diairo = divide and metro = measure) of a circle is any straight line segment that passes through the centre and whose endpoints are on the circular boundary, or, in more modern usage, the length of such a line segment. When using the word in the more modern sense, one speaks of the _____ rather than a _____, because all diameters of a circle have the same length. This length is twice the radius. The _____ of a circle is also the longest chord that the circle has.
   a. Thing
   b. Diameter0
   c. Undefined
   d. Undefined

174. Any point where a graph makes contact with an coordinate axis is called an _____ of the graph
   a. Intercept0
   b. Thing
   c. Undefined
   d. Undefined

175. _____ (or proportionality) are two quantities that vary in such a way that one of the quatities is a constant multiple of the other, or equivalently if they have a constant ratio.
   a. Thing
   b. Proportions0
   c. Undefined
   d. Undefined

176. In mathematics, a matrix can be thought of as each row or _____ being a vector. Hence, a space formed by row vectors or _____ vectors are said to be a row space or a _____ space.
   a. Column0
   b. Concept
   c. Undefined
   d. Undefined

177. _____ algebra (sometimes called General algebra) is the field of mathematics that studies the ideas common to all algebraic structures.
   a. Universal0
   b. Thing
   c. Undefined
   d. Undefined

178. A _____ models the S-curve of growth of some set P. The initial stage of growth is approximately exponential; then, as saturation begins, the growth slows, and at maturity, growth stops.
   a. Logistic function0
   b. Thing
   c. Undefined
   d. Undefined

179. Pierre François _____ was a mathematician and a doctor in number theory from the University of Ghent in 1825.
   a. Verhulst0
   b. Person
   c. Undefined
   d. Undefined

180. _____ is a state located in the southern and southwestern regions of the United States of America.
   a. Thing
   b. Texas0
   c. Undefined
   d. Undefined

181. In statistics the _____ of an event i is the number n_i of times the event occurred in the experiment or the study. These frequencies are often graphically represented in histograms.
   a. Frequency0
   b. Concept
   c. Undefined
   d. Undefined

Chapter 1. PREVIEW AND REVIEW

182. A _____ consists either of a suggested explanation for a phenomenon or of a reasoned proposal suggesting a possible correlation between multiple phenomena.
   a. Thing
   b. Hypothesis0
   c. Undefined
   d. Undefined

183. _____ generally, is the synthesis of triose phospates and ultimately starch, glucose and other products from sunlight, carbon dioxide and water.
   a. Thing
   b. Photosynthesis0
   c. Undefined
   d. Undefined

184. _____ interest refers to the fact that whenever interest is calculated, it is based not only on the original principal, but also on any unpaid interest that has been added to the principal.
   a. Thing
   b. Compound0
   c. Undefined
   d. Undefined

185. In mathematical analysis, _____ are objects which generalize functions and probability distributions.
   a. Thing
   b. Distribution0
   c. Undefined
   d. Undefined

186. The _____ of a geographic location is its height above a fixed reference point, often the mean sea level.
   a. Elevation0
   b. Thing
   c. Undefined
   d. Undefined

187. In vector calculus, the _____ of a scalar field is a vector field which points in the direction of the greatest rate of increase of the scalar field, and whose magnitude is the greatest rate of change.
   a. Thing
   b. Gradient0
   c. Undefined
   d. Undefined

188. In topology and related areas of mathematics a _____ or Moore-Smith sequence is a generalization of a sequence, intended to unify the various notions of limit and generalize them to arbitrary topological spaces.
   a. Net0
   b. Thing
   c. Undefined
   d. Undefined

189. The State of _____ is a state located in the Rocky Mountain region of the United States of America.
   a. Colorado0
   b. Thing
   c. Undefined
   d. Undefined

190. _____ (Groups, Algorithms and Programming) is a computer algebra system for computational discrete algebra with particular emphasis on, but not restricted to, computational group theory.
   a. Gap0
   b. Thing
   c. Undefined
   d. Undefined

191. In mathematics, the _____ , or members of a set or more generally a class are all those objects which when collected together make up the set or class.

a. Thing
b. Elements0
c. Undefined
d. Undefined

192. _____, also known as _____ of Alexandria, was a Greek mathematician. His Elements is the most successful textbook in the history of mathematics. In it, the principles of geometry are deduced from a small set of axioms. His method of proving mathematical theorems by logical reasoning from accepted first principles remains the backbone of mathematics and is responsible for the field's characteristic rigor
   a. Euclid0
   b. Person
   c. Undefined
   d. Undefined

193. _____ is the study of terms and their use — of words and compound words that are used in specific contexts.
   a. Thing
   b. Terminology0
   c. Undefined
   d. Undefined

194. Compass and straightedge or ruler-and-compass _____ is the _____ of lengths or angles using only an idealized ruler and compass.
   a. Thing
   b. Construction0
   c. Undefined
   d. Undefined

195. In mathematics, a _____ is the set of all points in three-dimensional space (R^3) which are at distance r from a fixed point of that space, where r is a positive real number called the radius of the _____. The fixed point is called the center or centre, and is not part of the _____ itself.
   a. Sphere0
   b. Thing
   c. Undefined
   d. Undefined

196. The _____ is the period of time required for a quantity to double in size or value.
   a. Doubling time0
   b. Thing
   c. Undefined
   d. Undefined

197. In abstract algebra, _____ consists of sets with binary operations that satisfy certain axioms.
   a. Grouping0
   b. Thing
   c. Undefined
   d. Undefined

198. A _____ is a movement of an object in a circular motion. A two-dimensional object rotates around a center (or point) of _____. A three-dimensional object rotates around a line called an axis. If the axis of _____ is within the body, the body is said to rotate upon itself, or spin—which implies relative speed and perhaps free-movement with angular momentum. A circular motion about an external point, e.g. the Earth about the Sun, is called an orbit or more properly an orbital revolution.
   a. Rotation0
   b. Thing
   c. Undefined
   d. Undefined

199. _____ is the chance that something is likely to happen or be the case.
   a. Probability0
   b. Thing
   c. Undefined
   d. Undefined

200. In the scientific method, an _____ (Latin: ex-+-periri, "of (or from) trying"), is a set of actions and observations, performed in the context of solving a particular problem or question, in order to support or falsify a hypothesis or research concerning phenomena.
   a. Thing
   b. Experiment0
   c. Undefined
   d. Undefined

201. _____ is a measure of the acidity or alkalinity of a solution.
   a. PH level0
   b. Thing
   c. Undefined
   d. Undefined

202. A _____ defined function $f(x)$ of a real variable x is a function whose definition is given differently on disjoint subsets of its domain.
   a. Piecewise0
   b. Thing
   c. Undefined
   d. Undefined

203. _____ the expected value of a random variable displays the average or central value of the variable. It is a summary value of the distribution of the variable.
   a. Thing
   b. Determining0
   c. Undefined
   d. Undefined

204. _____ is a means of calculating the volume of a solid of revolution, when integrating along the axis of revolution. This method models the generated 3 dimensional shape as a "stack" of an infinite number of disks of infinitesimal thickness.
   a. Thing
   b. Disk method0
   c. Undefined
   d. Undefined

Chapter 2. DISCRETE TIME MODELS, SEQUENCES, AND DIFFERENCE EQUATIONS

1. _____ are the basic objects of study in graph theory. Informally speaking, a graph is a set of objects called points, nodes, or vertices connected by links called lines or edges.
   a. Thing
   b. Graphs0
   c. Undefined
   d. Undefined

2. The mathematical concept of a _____ expresses the intuitive idea of deterministic dependence between two quantities, one of which is viewed as primary and the other as secondary. A _____ then is a way to associate a unique output for each input of a specified type, for example, a real number or an element of a given set.
   a. Thing
   b. Function0
   c. Undefined
   d. Undefined

3. The _____ of measurement are a globally standardized and modernized form of the metric system.
   a. Thing
   b. Units0
   c. Undefined
   d. Undefined

4. A _____ is a function that assigns a number to subsets of a given set.
   a. Thing
   b. Measure0
   c. Undefined
   d. Undefined

5. In sociology and biology a _____ is the collection of people or organisms of a particular species living in a given geographic area or space, usually measured by a census.
   a. Thing
   b. Population0
   c. Undefined
   d. Undefined

6. _____ are a measure of time.
   a. Thing
   b. Minutes0
   c. Undefined
   d. Undefined

7. The _____ integers are all the integers from zero on upwards.
   a. Thing
   b. Nonnegative0
   c. Undefined
   d. Undefined

8. Mathematical _____ is used to represent ideas.
   a. Thing
   b. Notation0
   c. Undefined
   d. Undefined

9. A _____ is a number, figure, or indicator that appears below the normal line of type, typically used in a formula, mathematical expression, or description of a chemical compound.
   a. Thing
   b. Subscript0
   c. Undefined
   d. Undefined

10. In mathematics and the mathematical sciences, a _____ is a fixed, but possibly unspecified, value. This is in contrast to a variable, which is not fixed.
    a. Thing
    b. Constant0
    c. Undefined
    d. Undefined

Chapter 2. DISCRETE TIME MODELS, SEQUENCES, AND DIFFERENCE EQUATIONS

11. In mathematics, _____ growth occurs when the growth rate of a function is always proportional to the function's current size.
    a. Thing
    b. Exponential0
    c. Undefined
    d. Undefined

12. _____ is one of the most important functions in mathematics. A function commonly used to study growth and decay
    a. Thing
    b. Exponential function0
    c. Undefined
    d. Undefined

13. In mathematics, a _____ may be described informally as a number that can be given by an infinite decimal representation.
    a. Real number0
    b. Thing
    c. Undefined
    d. Undefined

14. The _____ are the only integral domain whose positive elements are well-ordered, and in which order is preserved by addition. Like the natural numbers, the _____ form a countably infinite set. The set of all _____ is usually denoted in mathematics by a boldface Z .
    a. Thing
    b. Integers0
    c. Undefined
    d. Undefined

15. In mathematics, a _____ of a k-place relation $L \subseteq X_1 \times ... \times X_k$ is one of the sets X_j, $1 \le j \le k$. In the special case where k = 2 and $L \subseteq X_1 \times X_2$ is a function $L : X_1 \to X_2$, it is conventional to refer to X_1 as the _____ of the function and to refer to X_2 as the codomain of the function.
    a. Thing
    b. Domain0
    c. Undefined
    d. Undefined

16. Initial objects are also called _____, and terminal objects are also called final.
    a. Coterminal0
    b. Thing
    c. Undefined
    d. Undefined

17. In economics, economic _____ is simply a state of the world where economic forces are balanced and in the absence of external influences the values of economic variables will not change.
    a. Equilibrium0
    b. Thing
    c. Undefined
    d. Undefined

18. _____ is a method of defining functions in which the function being defined is applied within its own definition. The term is also used more generally to describe a process of repeating objects in a self-similar way.
    a. Recursion0
    b. Thing
    c. Undefined
    d. Undefined

19. Equivalence is the condition of being _____ or essentially equal.
    a. Equivalent0
    b. Thing
    c. Undefined
    d. Undefined

20. An _____ is a straight line around which a geometric figure can be rotated.

Chapter 2. DISCRETE TIME MODELS, SEQUENCES, AND DIFFERENCE EQUATIONS

a. Axis0
b. Thing
c. Undefined
d. Undefined

21. In astronomy, geography, geometry and related sciences and contexts, a plane is said to be _____ at a given point if it is locally perpendicular to the gradient of the gravity field, i.e., with the direction of the gravitational force at that point.
   a. Horizontal0
   b. Thing
   c. Undefined
   d. Undefined

22. A _____ consists of one quarter of the coordinate plane.
   a. Thing
   b. Quadrant0
   c. Undefined
   d. Undefined

23. _____ is often used to describe the measurement of the steepness, incline, gradient, or grade of a straight line. The _____ is defined as the ratio of the "rise" divided by the "run" between two points on a line, or in other words, the ratio of the altitude change to the horizontal distance between any two points on the line.
   a. Thing
   b. Slope0
   c. Undefined
   d. Undefined

24. In mathematics, the _____ of a coordinate system is the point where the axes of the system intersect.
   a. Origin0
   b. Thing
   c. Undefined
   d. Undefined

25. In mathematics, _____ occurs when the growth rate of a function is always proportional to the function's current size.
   a. Exponential growth0
   b. Thing
   c. Undefined
   d. Undefined

26. A _____ is a quantity that denotes the proportional amount or magnitude of one quantity relative to another.
   a. Thing
   b. Ratio0
   c. Undefined
   d. Undefined

27. _____ is mass m per unit volume V.
   a. Density0
   b. Thing
   c. Undefined
   d. Undefined

28. In mathematics, a _____ is an n-tuple with n being 3.
   a. Triple0
   b. Thing
   c. Undefined
   d. Undefined

29. A _____ is a set of numbers that designate location in a given reference system, such as x,y in a planar _____ system or an x,y,z in a three-dimensional _____ system.
   a. Thing
   b. Coordinate0
   c. Undefined
   d. Undefined

30. In mathematics and its applications, a _____ is a system for assigning an n-tuple of numbers or scalars to each point in an n-dimensional space.

Chapter 2. DISCRETE TIME MODELS, SEQUENCES, AND DIFFERENCE EQUATIONS

a. Coordinate system0
b. Concept
c. Undefined
d. Undefined

31. In mathematics, a _____ is a two-dimensional manifold or surface that is perfectly flat.
a. Plane0
b. Thing
c. Undefined
d. Undefined

32. In mathematics, a _____ is an ordered list of objects. Like a set, it contains members, also called elements or terms, and the number of terms is called the length of the _____. Unlike a set, order matters, and the exact same elements can appear multiple times at different positions in the _____.
a. Thing
b. Sequence0
c. Undefined
d. Undefined

33. _____ Any process by which a specified characteristic usually amplitude of the output of a device is prevented from exceeding a predetermined value.
a. Limiting0
b. Thing
c. Undefined
d. Undefined

34. _____ is change in population over time, and can be quantified as the change in the number of individuals in a population per unit time.
a. Population growth0
b. Thing
c. Undefined
d. Undefined

35. The word _____ comes from the 15th Century Latin word discretus which means separate.
a. Thing
b. Discrete0
c. Undefined
d. Undefined

36. In mathematics, when a method of defining functions is utilized, in which the function being defined is applied within its own definition, that pertaining function is called _____.
a. Thing
b. Recursive0
c. Undefined
d. Undefined

37. _____ is the state of being greater than any finite number, however large.
a. Thing
b. Infinity0
c. Undefined
d. Undefined

38. _____ denotes the approach toward a definite value, as time goes on; or to a definite point, a common view or opinion, or toward a fixed or equilibrium state.
a. Thing
b. Convergence0
c. Undefined
d. Undefined

39. The _____, the average in everyday English, which is also called the arithmetic _____ (and is distinguished from the geometric _____ or harmonic _____). The average is also called the sample _____. The expected value of a random variable, which is also called the population _____.

Chapter 2. DISCRETE TIME MODELS, SEQUENCES, AND DIFFERENCE EQUATIONS 27

    a. Thing
    b. Mean0
    c. Undefined
    d. Undefined

40. In elementary algebra, an _____ is a set that contains every real number between two indicated numbers and may contain the two numbers themselves.
    a. Interval0
    b. Thing
    c. Undefined
    d. Undefined

41. In mathematics, _____ describes an entity with a limit.
    a. Convergent0
    b. Thing
    c. Undefined
    d. Undefined

42. In mathematics, a _____ series is an infinite series that is not convergent, meaning that the infinite sequence of the partial sums of the series does not have a limit.
    a. Thing
    b. Divergent0
    c. Undefined
    d. Undefined

43. In mathematics, an _____ is a statement about the relative size or order of two objects.
    a. Inequality0
    b. Thing
    c. Undefined
    d. Undefined

44. In mathematics, a _____ is a demonstration that, assuming certain axioms, some statement is necessarily true.
    a. Thing
    b. Proof0
    c. Undefined
    d. Undefined

45. A _____ is a numeral used to indicate a count. The most common use of the word today is to name the part of a fraction that tells the number or count of equal parts.
    a. Thing
    b. Numerator0
    c. Undefined
    d. Undefined

46. _____ has many meanings, most of which simply .
    a. Thing
    b. Power0
    c. Undefined
    d. Undefined

47. A _____ is the part of a fraction that tells how many equal parts make up a whole, and which is used in the name of the fraction: "halves", "thirds", "fourths" or "quarters", "fifths" and so on.
    a. Concept
    b. Denominator0
    c. Undefined
    d. Undefined

48. A _____ is 360° or 2δ radians.
    a. Turn0
    b. Thing
    c. Undefined
    d. Undefined

49. The deductive-nomological model is a formalized view of scientific _____ in natural language.

Chapter 2. DISCRETE TIME MODELS, SEQUENCES, AND DIFFERENCE EQUATIONS

a. Explanation0
b. Thing
c. Undefined
d. Undefined

50. An _____ is a combination of numbers, operators, grouping symbols and/or free variables and bound variables arranged in a meaningful way which can be evaluated..
   a. Expression0
   b. Thing
   c. Undefined
   d. Undefined

51. _____ is essentially exponential growth based on a constant rate of compound interest.
   a. Thing
   b. Exponential growth model0
   c. Undefined
   d. Undefined

52. In mathematics, the concept of a _____ tries to capture the intuitive idea of a geometrical one-dimensional and continuous object. A simple example is the circle.
   a. Curve0
   b. Thing
   c. Undefined
   d. Undefined

53. In mathematics, an inequality is a statement about the relative size or order of two objects. For example 14 > 10, or 14 is _____ 10.
   a. Greater than0
   b. Thing
   c. Undefined
   d. Undefined

54. In mathematics, _____ refers to the rewriting of an expression into a simpler form.
   a. Thing
   b. Reduction0
   c. Undefined
   d. Undefined

55. A _____ is the quantity that defines certain relatively constant characteristics of systems or functions..
   a. Parameter0
   b. Thing
   c. Undefined
   d. Undefined

56. A _____ is a symbolic representation denoting a quantity or expression. It often represents an "unknown" quantity that has the potential to change.
   a. Variable0
   b. Thing
   c. Undefined
   d. Undefined

57. _____ is the estimation of a physical quantity such as distance, energy, temperature, or time.
   a. Measurement0
   b. Thing
   c. Undefined
   d. Undefined

58. In mathematics, the _____ is a conic section generated by the intersection of a right circular conical surface and a plane parallel to a generating straight line of that surface. It can also be defined as locus of points in a plane which are equidistant from a given point.
   a. Thing
   b. Parabola0
   c. Undefined
   d. Undefined

Chapter 2. DISCRETE TIME MODELS, SEQUENCES, AND DIFFERENCE EQUATIONS

59. In business, particularly accounting, a _____ is the time intervals that the accounts, statement, payments, or other calculations cover.
   a. Thing
   b. Period0
   c. Undefined
   d. Undefined

60. In mathematics, a _____ function in the sense of algebraic geometry is an everywhere-defined, polynomial function on an algebraic variety V with values in the field K over which V is defined.
   a. Thing
   b. Regular0
   c. Undefined
   d. Undefined

61. _____ is the ability to hold, receive or absorb, or a measure thereof, similar to the concept of volume.
   a. Capacity0
   b. Concept
   c. Undefined
   d. Undefined

62. _____ usually refers to the biological _____ of a population level that can be supported for an organism, given the quantity of food, habitat, water and other life infrastructure present.
   a. Thing
   b. Carrying capacity0
   c. Undefined
   d. Undefined

63. Leonardo of Pisa (1170s or 1180s – 1250), also known as Leonardo Pisano, Leonardo Bonacci, Leonardo _____, or, most commonly, simply _____, was an Italian mathematician, considered by some "the most talented mathematician of the Middle Ages."
   a. Person
   b. Fibonacci0
   c. Undefined
   d. Undefined

64. In mathematics, the conjugate _____ or adjoint matrix of an m-by-n matrix A with complex entries is the n-by-m matrix A* obtained from A by taking the transpose and then taking the complex conjugate of each entry.
   a. Thing
   b. Pairs0
   c. Undefined
   d. Undefined

65. In mathematics, a _____ is a polynomial equation of the second degree. The general form is $ax^2 + bx + c = 0$.
   a. Quadratic equation0
   b. Thing
   c. Undefined
   d. Undefined

66. Generally, in mathematics, a _____ of an object is a standard presentation.
   a. Canonical form0
   b. Thing
   c. Undefined
   d. Undefined

67. The _____ of a ring R is defined to be the smallest positive integer n such that n a = 0, for all a in R.
   a. Characteristic0
   b. Thing
   c. Undefined
   d. Undefined

68. In Euclidean geometry, a uniform _____ is a linear transformation that enlargers or diminishes objects, and whose _____ factor is the same in all directions. This is also called homothethy.

30 *Chapter 2. DISCRETE TIME MODELS, SEQUENCES, AND DIFFERENCE EQUATIONS*

    a. Scale0
    b. Thing
    c. Undefined
    d. Undefined

69. In mathematics, the _____ of two sets A and B is the set that contains all elements of A that also belong to B (or equivalently, all elements of B that also belong to A), but no other elements.
    a. Intersection0
    b. Thing
    c. Undefined
    d. Undefined

70. _____ is a synonym for information.
    a. Data0
    b. Thing
    c. Undefined
    d. Undefined

71. _____ or arithmetics is the oldest and most elementary branch of mathematics, used by almost everyone, for tasks ranging from simple daily counting to advanced science and business calculations.
    a. Thing
    b. Arithmetic0
    c. Undefined
    d. Undefined

72. _____ of a list of numbers is the sum of all the members of the list divided by the number of items in the list.
    a. Arithmetic mean0
    b. Thing
    c. Undefined
    d. Undefined

Chapter 3. LIMITS AND CONTINUITY

1. In Euclidean geometry, a uniform _____ is a linear transformation that enlargers or diminishes objects, and whose _____ factor is the same in all directions. This is also called homothethy.
   a. Thing
   b. Scale0
   c. Undefined
   d. Undefined

2. In sociology and biology a _____ is the collection of people or organisms of a particular species living in a given geographic area or space, usually measured by a census.
   a. Population0
   b. Thing
   c. Undefined
   d. Undefined

3. In elementary algebra, an _____ is a set that contains every real number between two indicated numbers and may contain the two numbers themselves.
   a. Interval0
   b. Thing
   c. Undefined
   d. Undefined

4. A _____ is a symbolic representation denoting a quantity or expression. It often represents an "unknown" quantity that has the potential to change.
   a. Variable0
   b. Thing
   c. Undefined
   d. Undefined

5. In trigonometry, the _____ is a function defined as $\tan x = \sin x / \cos x$. The function is so-named because it can be defined as the length of a certain segment of a _____ (in the geometric sense) to the unit circle. In plane geometry, a line is _____ to a curve, at some point, if both line and curve pass through the point with the same direction.
   a. Tangent0
   b. Thing
   c. Undefined
   d. Undefined

6. _____ has two distinct but etymologically-related meanings: one in geometry and one in trigonometry.
   a. Tangent line0
   b. Thing
   c. Undefined
   d. Undefined

7. _____ is a trigonometric function that is the reciprocal of cosine.
   a. Secant0
   b. Thing
   c. Undefined
   d. Undefined

8. _____ of a curve is a line that intersects two or more points on the curve.
   a. Secant line0
   b. Thing
   c. Undefined
   d. Undefined

9. In mathematics, a set is called _____ if there is a bijection between the set and some set of the form {1, 2, ..., n} where n is a natural number.
   a. Finite0
   b. Thing
   c. Undefined
   d. Undefined

10. The _____, the average in everyday English, which is also called the arithmetic _____ (and is distinguished from the geometric _____ or harmonic _____). The average is also called the sample _____. The expected value of a random variable, which is also called the population _____.

Chapter 3. LIMITS AND CONTINUITY

   a. Thing
   b. Mean0
   c. Undefined
   d. Undefined

11. Mathematical _____ is used to represent ideas.
   a. Thing
   b. Notation0
   c. Undefined
   d. Undefined

12. In mathematics, an inequality is a statement about the relative size or order of two objects. For example 14 > 10, or 14 is _____ 10.
   a. Greater than0
   b. Thing
   c. Undefined
   d. Undefined

13. A _____ is the part of a fraction that tells how many equal parts make up a whole, and which is used in the name of the fraction: "halves", "thirds", "fourths" or "quarters", "fifths" and so on.
   a. Denominator0
   b. Concept
   c. Undefined
   d. Undefined

14. In mathematics, a _____ of a k-place relation $L \subseteq X_1 \times ... \times X_k$ is one of the sets X_j, $1 \leq j \leq k$. In the special case where k = 2 and $L \subseteq X_1 \times X_2$ is a function $L : X_1 \rightarrow X_2$, it is conventional to refer to X_1 as the _____ of the function and to refer to X_2 as the codomain of the function.
   a. Thing
   b. Domain0
   c. Undefined
   d. Undefined

15. _____ are objects, characters, or other concrete representations of ideas, concepts, or other abstractions.
   a. Symbols0
   b. Thing
   c. Undefined
   d. Undefined

16. The mathematical concept of a _____ expresses the intuitive idea of deterministic dependence between two quantities, one of which is viewed as primary and the other as secondary. A _____ then is a way to associate a unique output for each input of a specified type, for example, a real number or an element of a given set.
   a. Function0
   b. Thing
   c. Undefined
   d. Undefined

17. _____ is an operator that measures the magnitude of a vector field's source or sink at a given point; the _____ of a vector field is a signed scalar.
   a. Thing
   b. Divergence0
   c. Undefined
   d. Undefined

18. In mathematics, a _____ number is a number which can be expressed as a ratio of two integers. Non-integer _____ numbers (commonly called fractions) are usually written as the vulgar fraction a / b, where b is not zero.
   a. Thing
   b. Rational0
   c. Undefined
   d. Undefined

19. In mathematics, a _____ is any function which can be written as the ratio of two polynomial functions.

Chapter 3. LIMITS AND CONTINUITY

a. Thing
b. Rational function0
c. Undefined
d. Undefined

20. In mathematics, a _____ is an expression that is constructed from one or more variables and constants, using only the operations of addition, subtraction, multiplication, and constant positive whole number exponents. is a _____. Note in particular that division by an expression containing a variable is not in general allowed in polynomials. [1]
    a. Thing
    b. Polynomial0
    c. Undefined
    d. Undefined

21. A _____ is a numeral used to indicate a count. The most common use of the word today is to name the part of a fraction that tells the number or count of equal parts.
    a. Numerator0
    b. Thing
    c. Undefined
    d. Undefined

22. A _____ is a negotiable instrument instructing a financial institution to pay a specific amount of a specific currency from a specific demand account held in the maker/depositor's name with that institution. Both the maker and payee may be natural persons or legal entities.
    a. Thing
    b. Check0
    c. Undefined
    d. Undefined

23. A _____ function is a function for which, intuitively, small changes in the input result in small changes in the output.
    a. Continuous0
    b. Event
    c. Undefined
    d. Undefined

24. In Euclidean geometry, a _____ is the set of all points in a plane at a fixed distance, called the radius, from a given point, the center.
    a. Circle0
    b. Thing
    c. Undeflned
    d. Undeflned

25. In geometry, an _____ is a point at which a line segment or ray terminates.
    a. Endpoint0
    b. Thing
    c. Undefined
    d. Undefined

26. Continuous functions are of utmost importance in mathematics and applications. However, not all functions are continuous. If a function is not continuous at a point in its domain, one says that it has a _____ there. The set of all points of _____ of a function may be a discrete set, a dense set, or even the entire domain of the function.
    a. Thing
    b. Discontinuity0
    c. Undefined
    d. Undefined

27. In common philosophical language, a proposition or _____, is the content of an assertion, that is, it is true-or-false and defined by the meaning of a particular piece of language.
    a. Statement0
    b. Concept
    c. Undefined
    d. Undefined

Chapter 3. LIMITS AND CONTINUITY

28. In mathematics, the _____ functions are functions of an angle; they are important when studying triangles and modeling periodic phenomena, among many other applications.
    a. Thing
    b. Trigonometric0
    c. Undefined
    d. Undefined

29. _____ has many meanings, most of which simply .
    a. Thing
    b. Power0
    c. Undefined
    d. Undefined

30. In mathematics, _____ growth occurs when the growth rate of a function is always proportional to the function's current size.
    a. Thing
    b. Exponential0
    c. Undefined
    d. Undefined

31. _____ is one of the most important functions in mathematics. A function commonly used to study growth and decay
    a. Thing
    b. Exponential function0
    c. Undefined
    d. Undefined

32. In mathematics, a _____ is a statement that can be proved on the basis of explicitly stated or previously agreed assumptions.
    a. Theorem0
    b. Thing
    c. Undefined
    d. Undefined

33. In mathematics, the _____ of a function is the set of all "output" values produced by that function. Given a function $f : A \to B$, the _____ of f, is defined to be the set $\{x \in B : x = f(a) \text{ for some } a \in A\}$.
    a. Thing
    b. Range0
    c. Undefined
    d. Undefined

34. _____ is the state of being greater than any finite number, however large.
    a. Thing
    b. Infinity0
    c. Undefined
    d. Undefined

35. _____ Any process by which a specified characteristic usually amplitude of the output of a device is prevented from exceeding a predetermined value.
    a. Thing
    b. Limiting0
    c. Undefined
    d. Undefined

36. In mathematics, defined and _____ are used to explain whether or not expressions have meaningful, sensible, and unambiguous values.
    a. Undefined0
    b. Thing
    c. Undefined
    d. Undefined

37. A _____ is a quantity that denotes the proportional amount or magnitude of one quantity relative to another.

Chapter 3. LIMITS AND CONTINUITY

    a. Ratio0   b. Thing
    c. Undefined   d. Undefined

38. In mathematics, a _____ may be described informally as a number that can be given by an infinite decimal representation.
    a. Real number0   b. Thing
    c. Undefined   d. Undefined

39. In mathematics, a _____ is a constant multiplicative factor of a certain object. The object can be such things as a variable, a vector, a function, etc. For example, the _____ of $9x^2$ is 9.
    a. Coefficient0   b. Thing
    c. Undefined   d. Undefined

40. In mathematics, there are several meanings of _____ depending on the subject.
    a. Thing   b. Degree0
    c. Undefined   d. Undefined

41. An _____ is a combination of numbers, operators, grouping symbols and/or free variables and bound variables arranged in a meaningful way which can be evaluated..
    a. Expression0   b. Thing
    c. Undefined   d. Undefined

42. A _____ is a special kind of ratio, indicating a relationship between two measurements with different units, such as miles to gallons or cents to pounds.
    a. Rate0   b. Thing
    c. Undefined   d. Undefined

43. In mathematics, the concept of a _____ tries to capture the intuitive idea of a geometrical one-dimensional and continuous object. A simple example is the circle.
    a. Thing   b. Curve0
    c. Undefined   d. Undefined

44. A _____ models the S-curve of growth of some set P. The initial stage of growth is approximately exponential; then, as saturation begins, the growth slows, and at maturity, growth stops.
    a. Thing   b. Logistic function0
    c. Undefined   d. Undefined

45. _____ is mass m per unit volume V.
    a. Density0   b. Thing
    c. Undefined   d. Undefined

46. A _____ is the quantity that defines certain relatively constant characteristics of systems or functions..
    a. Thing   b. Parameter0
    c. Undefined   d. Undefined

47. _____ of an object is its speed in a particular direction.

a. Thing
b. Velocity0
c. Undefined
d. Undefined

48. Initial objects are also called _____, and terminal objects are also called final.
a. Coterminal0
b. Thing
c. Undefined
d. Undefined

49. A _____ is a set of numbers that designate location in a given reference system, such as x,y in a planar _____ system or an x,y,z in a three-dimensional _____ system.
a. Thing
b. Coordinate0
c. Undefined
d. Undefined

50. In mathematics and its applications, a _____ is a system for assigning an n-tuple of numbers or scalars to each point in an n-dimensional space.
a. Coordinate system0
b. Concept
c. Undefined
d. Undefined

51. In mathematics and its applications, _____ are used for assigning an n-tuple of numbers or scalars to each point in an n-dimensional space.
a. Coordinate systems0
b. Concept
c. Undefined
d. Undefined

52. In calculus, the _____ is a theorem regarding the limit of a function. The theorem asserts that if two functions approach the same limit at a point, and if a third function is "squeezed" between those functions, then the third function also approaches that limit at that point.
a. Squeeze Theorem0
b. Thing
c. Undefined
d. Undefined

53. In mathematics, a _____ is the result of multiplying, or an expression that identifies factors to be multiplied.
a. Product0
b. Thing
c. Undefined
d. Undefined

54. In mathematics, factorization (British English: factorisation) or factoring is the decomposition of an object (for example, a number, a polynomial, or a matrix) into a product of other objects, or _____, which when multiplied together give the original.
a. Thing
b. Factors0
c. Undefined
d. Undefined

55. The _____ are functions of an angle; they are important when studying triangles and modeling periodic phenomena, among many other applications.
a. Thing
b. Trigonometric functions0
c. Undefined
d. Undefined

56. _____ are the basic objects of study in graph theory. Informally speaking, a graph is a set of objects called points, nodes, or vertices connected by links called lines or edges.

Chapter 3. LIMITS AND CONTINUITY

  a. Thing
  c. Undefined
  b. Graphs0
  d. Undefined

57. _____ is a mathematical subject that includes the study of limits, derivatives, integrals, and power series and constitutes a major part of modern university curriculum.
  a. Thing
  c. Undefined
  b. Calculus0
  d. Undefined

58. A _____ is traditionally an infinitesimally small change in a variable.
  a. Thing
  c. Undefined
  b. Differential0
  d. Undefined

59. _____, a field in mathematics, is the study of how functions change when their inputs change. The primary object of study in _____ is the derivative.
  a. Differential calculus0
  c. Undefined
  b. Thing
  d. Undefined

60. In mathematics, a _____ is a demonstration that, assuming certain axioms, some statement is necessarily true.
  a. Proof0
  c. Undefined
  b. Thing
  d. Undefined

61. In mathematics, science including computer science, linguistics and engineering, an _____ is, generally speaking, an independent variable or input to a function.
  a. Thing
  c. Undefined
  b. Argument0
  d. Undefined

62. In mathematics, an _____ is a statement about the relative size or order of two objects.
  a. Inequallty0
  c. Undefined
  b. ThIng
  d. Undefined

63. A _____ is one of the basic shapes of geometry: a polygon with three vertices and three sides which are straight line segments.
  a. Thing
  c. Undefined
  b. Triangle0
  d. Undefined

64. _____ is a circle with a unit radius, i.e., a circle whose radius is 1.
  a. Unit circle0
  c. Undefined
  b. Thing
  d. Undefined

65. The _____ is a unit of plane angle. It is represented by the symbol "rad" or, more rarely, by the superscript c (for "circular measure"). For example, an angle of 1.2 radians would be written "1.2 rad" or "1.2c" (second symbol can produce confusion with centigrads).
  a. Thing
  c. Undefined
  b. Radian0
  d. Undefined

66. In Euclidean geometry, an _____ is a closed segment of a differentiable curve in the two-dimensional plane; for example, a circular _____ is a segment of a circle.
   a. Concept
   b. Arc0
   c. Undefined
   d. Undefined

67. A circular _____ or circle _____ also known as a pie piece is the portion of a circle enclosed by two radii and an arc.
   a. Thing
   b. Sector0
   c. Undefined
   d. Undefined

68. _____ is an adjective usually refering to being in the centre.
   a. Thing
   b. Central0
   c. Undefined
   d. Undefined

69. In classical geometry, a _____ of a circle or sphere is any line segment from its center to its boundary. By extension, the _____ of a circle or sphere is the length of any such segment. The _____ is half the diameter. In science and engineering the term _____ of curvature is commonly used as a synonym for _____.
   a. Radius0
   b. Thing
   c. Undefined
   d. Undefined

70. _____ also called rectification of a curve—was historically difficult.
   a. Arc length0
   b. Thing
   c. Undefined
   d. Undefined

71. An _____ is an equality that remains true regardless of the values of any variables that appear within it, to distinguish it from an equality which is true under more particular conditions.
   a. Thing
   b. Identity0
   c. Undefined
   d. Undefined

72. A _____ is a landform that extends above the surrounding terrain in a limited area. A _____ is generally steeper than a hill, but there is no universally accepted standard definition for the height of a _____ or a hill although a _____ usually has an identifiable summit.
   a. Mountain0
   b. Thing
   c. Undefined
   d. Undefined

73. A _____ is a function for which, intuitively, small changes in the input result in small changes in the output.
   a. Event
   b. Continuous function0
   c. Undefined
   d. Undefined

74. The _____ of a geographic location is its height above a fixed reference point, often the mean sea level.
   a. Thing
   b. Elevation0
   c. Undefined
   d. Undefined

75. _____ is a physical property of a system that underlies the common notions of hot and cold; something that is hotter has the greater _____.

Chapter 3. LIMITS AND CONTINUITY

a. Temperature0
b. Thing
c. Undefined
d. Undefined

76. The _____ implies that on any great circle around the world, the temperature, pressure, elevation, carbon dioxide concentration, or anything else that varies continuously, there will always exist two antipodal points that share the same value for that variable.
    a. Intermediate Value Theorem0
    b. Thing
    c. Undefined
    d. Undefined

77. The _____ are the only integral domain whose positive elements are well-ordered, and in which order is preserved by addition. Like the natural numbers, the _____ form a countably infinite set. The set of all _____ is usually denoted in mathematics by a boldface Z .
    a. Integers0
    b. Thing
    c. Undefined
    d. Undefined

78. The _____ is a root-finding algorithm which works by repeatedly dividing an interval in half and then selecting the subinterval in which the root exists.
    a. Thing
    b. Bisection method0
    c. Undefined
    d. Undefined

79. In mathematics, a _____ of a complex-valued function f is a member x of the domain of f such that f(x) vanishes at x, that is, x : f (x) = 0.
    a. Root0
    b. Thing
    c. Undefined
    d. Undefined

80. _____ is the process of reducing the number of significant digits in a number.
    a. Concept
    b. Rounding0
    c. Undefined
    d. Undefined

81. _____ is the middle point of a line segment.
    a. Midpoint0
    b. Thing
    c. Undefined
    d. Undefined

82. A _____ is a function that assigns a number to subsets of a given set.
    a. Thing
    b. Measure0
    c. Undefined
    d. Undefined

83. _____ is the estimation of a physical quantity such as distance, energy, temperature, or time.
    a. Thing
    b. Measurement0
    c. Undefined
    d. Undefined

84. _____ is the fee paid on borrowed money.
    a. Interest0
    b. Thing
    c. Undefined
    d. Undefined

Chapter 3. LIMITS AND CONTINUITY

85. Sir Isaac _____, was an English physicist, mathematician, astronomer, natural philosopher, and alchemist, regarded by many as the greatest figure in the history of science
    a. Newton0
    b. Person
    c. Undefined
    d. Undefined

86. _____ was a German mathematician and philosopher. He invented calculus independently of Newton, and his notation is the one in general use since.
    a. Person
    b. Leibniz0
    c. Undefined
    d. Undefined

87. In mathematics, a _____ is a countable collection of open covers of a topological space that satisfies certain separation axioms.
    a. Thing
    b. Development0
    c. Undefined
    d. Undefined

88. The word _____ comes from the Latin word linearis, which means created by lines.
    a. Thing
    b. Linear0
    c. Undefined
    d. Undefined

89. In mathematics and the mathematical sciences, a _____ is a fixed, but possibly unspecified, value. This is in contrast to a variable, which is not fixed.
    a. Constant0
    b. Thing
    c. Undefined
    d. Undefined

90. In mathematics, especially in order theory, an _____ of a subset S of some partially ordered set is an element of P which is greater than or equal to every element of S.
    a. Upper bound0
    b. Thing
    c. Undefined
    d. Undefined

91. In geographic information systems, a _____ comprises an entity with a geographic location, typically determined by points, arcs, or polygons. Carriageways and cadastres exemplify _____ data.
    a. Thing
    b. Feature0
    c. Undefined
    d. Undefined

92. In mathematics, two quantities are called _____ if they vary in such a way that one of the quantities is a constant multiple of the other, or equivalently if they have a constant ratio.
    a. Thing
    b. Proportional0
    c. Undefined
    d. Undefined

93. In business, particularly accounting, a _____ is the time intervals that the accounts, statement, payments, or other calculations cover.
    a. Period0
    b. Thing
    c. Undefined
    d. Undefined

Chapter 3. LIMITS AND CONTINUITY

94. In banking and accountancy, the outstanding _____ is the amount of money owned, or due, that remains in a deposit account or a loan account at a given date, after all past remittances, payments and withdrawal have been accounted for.
    a. Thing
    b. Balance0
    c. Undefined
    d. Undefined

95. In economics _____ means before deductions brutto, e.g. _____ domestic or national product, or _____ profit or income
    a. Gross0
    b. Thing
    c. Undefined
    d. Undefined

96. A _____ is an analog of an ordinary trigonometric, or circular, function.
    a. Thing
    b. Hyperbolic function0
    c. Undefined
    d. Undefined

Chapter 4. DIFFERENTIATION

1. In trigonometry, the _____ is a function defined as tan x = $^{\sin x}/_{\cos x}$. The function is so-named because it can be defined as the length of a certain segment of a _____ (in the geometric sense) to the unit circle. In plane geometry, a line is _____ to a curve, at some point, if both line and curve pass through the point with the same direction.
   a. Tangent0
   b. Thing
   c. Undefined
   d. Undefined

2. _____ has two distinct but etymologically-related meanings: one in geometry and one in trigonometry.
   a. Thing
   b. Tangent line0
   c. Undefined
   d. Undefined

3. In mathematics, the concept of a _____ tries to capture the intuitive idea of a geometrical one-dimensional and continuous object. A simple example is the circle.
   a. Thing
   b. Curve0
   c. Undefined
   d. Undefined

4. _____ is a free computer algebra system based on a 1982 version of Macsyma
   a. Maxima0
   b. Thing
   c. Undefined
   d. Undefined

5. _____ are points in the domain of a function at which the function takes a largest value or smallest value, either within a given neighborhood or on the function domain in its entirety.
   a. Thing
   b. Maxima and minima0
   c. Undefined
   d. Undefined

6. _____ is a mathematical subject that includes the study of limits, derivatives, integrals, and power series and constitutes a major part of modern university curriculum.
   a. Calculus0
   b. Thing
   c. Undefined
   d. Undefined

7. A _____ is traditionally an infinitesimally small change in a variable.
   a. Differential0
   b. Thing
   c. Undefined
   d. Undefined

8. _____, a field in mathematics, is the study of how functions change when their inputs change. The primary object of study in _____ is the derivative.
   a. Thing
   b. Differential calculus0
   c. Undefined
   d. Undefined

9. In mathematics, maxima and _____, known collectively as extrema, are points in the domain of a function at which the function takes a largest value .
   a. Thing
   b. Minima0
   c. Undefined
   d. Undefined

10. When _____ symmetry one can determine whether or not an object is symmetric with respect to a given mathematical operation, if, when applied to the object, this operation does not change the object or its appearance.

Chapter 4. DIFFERENTIATION

a. Investigating0
b. Thing
c. Undefined
d. Undefined

11. In statistics the _____ of an event i is the number n_i of times the event occurred in the experiment or the study. These frequencies are often graphically represented in histograms.
   a. Frequency0
   b. Concept
   c. Undefined
   d. Undefined

12. _____ is the fee paid on borrowed money.
   a. Interest0
   b. Thing
   c. Undefined
   d. Undefined

13. _____ is a trigonometric function that is the reciprocal of cosine.
   a. Secant0
   b. Thing
   c. Undefined
   d. Undefined

14. _____ of a curve is a line that intersects two or more points on the curve.
   a. Secant line0
   b. Thing
   c. Undefined
   d. Undefined

15. A _____ is a special kind of ratio, indicating a relationship between two measurements with different units, such as miles to gallons or cents to pounds.
   a. Thing
   b. Rate0
   c. Undefined
   d. Undefined

16. _____ is often used to describe the measurement of the steepness, incline, gradient, or grade of a straight line. The _____ is defined as the ratio of the "rise" divided by the "run" between two points on a line, or in other words, the ratio of the altitude change to the horizontal distance between any two points on the line.
   a. Slope0
   b. Thing
   c. Undefined
   d. Undefined

17. The _____ is a measurement of how a function changes when the values of its inputs change.
   a. Thing
   b. Derivative0
   c. Undefined
   d. Undefined

18. The mathematical concept of a _____ expresses the intuitive idea of deterministic dependence between two quantities, one of which is viewed as primary and the other as secondary. A _____ then is a way to associate a unique output for each input of a specified type, for example, a real number or an element of a given set.
   a. Function0
   b. Thing
   c. Undefined
   d. Undefined

19. In geometry, an _____ is a point at which a line segment or ray terminates.
   a. Thing
   b. Endpoint0
   c. Undefined
   d. Undefined

Chapter 4. DIFFERENTIATION

20. In mathematics, a _____ is the end result of a division problem. It can also be expressed as the number of times the divisor divides into the dividend.
   a. Thing
   b. Quotient0
   c. Undefined
   d. Undefined

21. The function difference divided by the point difference is known as the _____
   a. Thing
   b. Difference quotient0
   c. Undefined
   d. Undefined

22. In elementary algebra, an _____ is a set that contains every real number between two indicated numbers and may contain the two numbers themselves.
   a. Interval0
   b. Thing
   c. Undefined
   d. Undefined

23. In astronomy, geography, geometry and related sciences and contexts, a plane is said to be _____ at a given point if it is locally perpendicular to the gradient of the gravity field, i.e., with the direction of the gravitational force at that point.
   a. Horizontal0
   b. Thing
   c. Undefined
   d. Undefined

24. In mathematics and the mathematical sciences, a _____ is a fixed, but possibly unspecified, value. This is in contrast to a variable, which is not fixed.
   a. Thing
   b. Constant0
   c. Undefined
   d. Undefined

25. _____ is a function whose values do not vary and thus are constant.
   a. Thing
   b. Constant function0
   c. Undefined
   d. Undefined

26. An _____ is a combination of numbers, operators, grouping symbols and/or free variables and bound variables arranged in a meaningful way which can be evaluated..
   a. Expression0
   b. Thing
   c. Undefined
   d. Undefined

27. The word _____ comes from the Latin word linearis, which means created by lines.
   a. Thing
   b. Linear0
   c. Undefined
   d. Undefined

28. A _____ is a first degree polynomial mathematical function of the form: f(x) = mx + b where m and b are real constants and x is a real variable.
   a. Linear function0
   b. Thing
   c. Undefined
   d. Undefined

29. _____ of an object is its speed in a particular direction.
   a. Thing
   b. Velocity0
   c. Undefined
   d. Undefined

Chapter 4. DIFFERENTIATION

30. In mathematics, an _____, mean, or central tendency of a data set refers to a measure of the "middle" or "expected" value of the data set.
   a. Concept
   b. Average0
   c. Undefined
   d. Undefined

31. A _____ is a quantity that denotes the proportional amount or magnitude of one quantity relative to another.
   a. Ratio0
   b. Thing
   c. Undefined
   d. Undefined

32. In mathematics, the additive inverse, or _____ of a number n is the number that, when added to n, yields zero. The additive inverse of n is denoted −n. For example, 7 is −7, because 7 + (−7) = 0, and the additive inverse of −0.3 is 0.3, because −0.3 + 0.3 = 0.
   a. Thing
   b. Opposite0
   c. Undefined
   d. Undefined

33. In mathematics, the _____ of a number n is the number that, when added to n, yields zero. The _____ of n is denoted −n. For example, 7 is −7, because 7 + (−7) = 0, and the _____ of −0.3 is 0.3, because −0.3 + 0.3 = 0.
   a. Thing
   b. Additive inverse0
   c. Undefined
   d. Undefined

34. In mathematics, the _____ (or modulus) of a real number is its numerical value without regard to its sign.
   a. Absolute value0
   b. Thing
   c. Undefined
   d. Undefined

35. A _____ is 360° or 2δ radians.
   a. Turn0
   b. Thing
   c. Undefined
   d. Undefined

36. A _____ is a mathematical equation for an unknown function of one or several variables which relates the values of the function itself and of its derivatives of various orders.
   a. Differential equation0
   b. Thing
   c. Undefined
   d. Undefined

37. The _____, the average in everyday English, which is also called the arithmetic _____ (and is distinguished from the geometric _____ or harmonic _____). The average is also called the sample _____. The expected value of a random variable, which is also called the population _____.
   a. Mean0
   b. Thing
   c. Undefined
   d. Undefined

38. In the scientific method, an _____ (Latin: ex-+-periri, "of (or from) trying"), is a set of actions and observations, performed in the context of solving a particular problem or question, in order to support or falsify a hypothesis or research concerning phenomena.
   a. Thing
   b. Experiment0
   c. Undefined
   d. Undefined

Chapter 4. DIFFERENTIATION

39. _____ Any process by which a specified characteristic usually amplitude of the output of a device is prevented from exceeding a predetermined value.
   a. Limiting0
   b. Thing
   c. Undefined
   d. Undefined

40. Acid _____ ratio measures the ability of a company to use its near cash or quick assets to immediately extinguish its current liabilities.
   a. Thing
   b. Test0
   c. Undefined
   d. Undefined

41. In mathematics, the word _____ is used informally to refer to certain distinct bodies of knowledge about mathematics.
   a. Theoretical0
   b. Thing
   c. Undefined
   d. Undefined

42. A _____ is a statement or claimt that a particular event will occur in the future in more certain terms than a forecast.
   a. Prediction0
   b. Thing
   c. Undefined
   d. Undefined

43. _____ is a state located in the Midwestern region of the United States of America.
   a. Minnesota0
   b. Thing
   c. Undefined
   d. Undefined

44. _____ are the basic objects of study in graph theory. Informally speaking, a graph is a set of objects called points, nodes, or vertices connected by links called lines or edges.
   a. Thing
   b. Graphs0
   c. Undefined
   d. Undefined

45. In _____ algebra, a *-ring is an associative ring with an antilinear, antiautomorphism * : A ¨ A which is an involution.
   a. Thing
   b. Star0
   c. Undefined
   d. Undefined

46. In banking and accountancy, the outstanding _____ is the amount of money owned, or due, that remains in a deposit account or a loan account at a given date, after all past remittances, payments and withdrawal have been accounted for.
   a. Thing
   b. Balance0
   c. Undefined
   d. Undefined

47. A _____ function is a function for which, intuitively, small changes in the input result in small changes in the output.
   a. Continuous0
   b. Event
   c. Undefined
   d. Undefined

Chapter 4. DIFFERENTIATION

48. In mathematics, a _____ is a statement that can be proved on the basis of explicitly stated or previously agreed assumptions.
   a. Theorem0
   b. Thing
   c. Undefined
   d. Undefined

49. In mathematics, a _____ is the result of multiplying, or an expression that identifies factors to be multiplied.
   a. Thing
   b. Product0
   c. Undefined
   d. Undefined

50. The _____ governs the differentiation of products of differentiable functions.
   a. Thing
   b. Product rule0
   c. Undefined
   d. Undefined

51. A _____ is a set of numbers that designate location in a given reference system, such as x,y in a planar _____ system or an x,y,z in a three-dimensional _____ system.
   a. Coordinate0
   b. Thing
   c. Undefined
   d. Undefined

52. In mathematics and its applications, a _____ is a system for assigning an n-tuple of numbers or scalars to each point in an n-dimensional space.
   a. Coordinate system0
   b. Concept
   c. Undefined
   d. Undefined

53. A _____ is a unit of length in the metric system, equal to one thousand metres, the current SI base unit of length
   a. Thing
   b. Kilometer0
   c. Undefined
   d. Undefined

54. The metre (or _____, see spelling differences) is a measure of length. It is the basic unit of length in the metric system and in the International System of Units (SI), used around the world for general and scientific purposes.
   a. Concept
   b. Meter0
   c. Undefined
   d. Undefined

55. In sociology and biology a _____ is the collection of people or organisms of a particular species living in a given geographic area or space, usually measured by a census.
   a. Thing
   b. Population0
   c. Undefined
   d. Undefined

56. In mathematics, the _____ of two sets A and B is the set that contains all elements of A that also belong to B (or equivalently, all elements of B that also belong to A), but no other elements.
   a. Thing
   b. Intersection0
   c. Undefined
   d. Undefined

57. A _____ is the quantity that defines certain relatively constant characteristics of systems or functions..
   a. Parameter0
   b. Thing
   c. Undefined
   d. Undefined

Chapter 4. DIFFERENTIATION

58. A _____ is a function that assigns a number to subsets of a given set.
    a. Thing
    b. Measure0
    c. Undefined
    d. Undefined

59. In mathematics, a _____ is an expression that is constructed from one or more variables and constants, using only the operations of addition, subtraction, multiplication, and constant positive whole number exponents. is a _____. Note in particular that division by an expression containing a variable is not in general allowed in polynomials. [1]
    a. Thing
    b. Polynomial0
    c. Undefined
    d. Undefined

60. _____ has many meanings, most of which simply .
    a. Thing
    b. Power0
    c. Undefined
    d. Undefined

61. _____ is a method for differentiating expressions involving exponentiation the power operation.
    a. Thing
    b. Power rule0
    c. Undefined
    d. Undefined

62. In mathematics, the _____ f is the collection of all ordered pairs . In particular, graph means the graphical representation of this collection, in the form of a curve or surface, together with axes, etc. Graphing on a Cartesian plane is sometimes referred to as curve sketching.
    a. Thing
    b. Graph of a function0
    c. Undefined
    d. Undefined

63. In mathematics, a _____ of a k-place relation $L \subseteq X_1 \times \ldots \times X_k$ is one of the sets X_j, $1 \leq j \leq k$. In the special case where k = 2 and $L \subseteq X_1 \times X_2$ is a function $L : X_1 \to X_2$, it is conventional to refer to X_1 as the _____ of the function and to refer to X_2 as the codomain of the function.
    a. Thing
    b. Domain0
    c. Undefined
    d. Undefined

64. A _____ is a numeral used to indicate a count. The most common use of the word today is to name the part of a fraction that tells the number or count of equal parts.
    a. Numerator0
    b. Thing
    c. Undefined
    d. Undefined

65. An _____ of a product of sums expresses it as a sum of products by using the fact that multiplication distributes over addition.
    a. Expansion0
    b. Thing
    c. Undefined
    d. Undefined

66. A _____ is the part of a fraction that tells how many equal parts make up a whole, and which is used in the name of the fraction: "halves", "thirds", "fourths" or "quarters", "fifths" and so on.
    a. Concept
    b. Denominator0
    c. Undefined
    d. Undefined

67. In mathematics, a _____ is a demonstration that, assuming certain axioms, some statement is necessarily true.

Chapter 4. DIFFERENTIATION

a. Proof0
b. Thing
c. Undefined
d. Undefined

68. The _____ are the only integral domain whose positive elements are well-ordered, and in which order is preserved by addition. Like the natural numbers, the _____ form a countably infinite set. The set of all _____ is usually denoted in mathematics by a boldface Z.

a. Integers0
b. Thing
c. Undefined
d. Undefined

69. A _____ is the result of the addition of a set of numbers. The numbers may be natural numbers, complex numbers, matrices, or still more complicated objects. An infinite _____ is a subtle procedure known as a series.

a. Thing
b. Sum0
c. Undefined
d. Undefined

70. In mathematics, the _____ is an important formula giving the expansion of powers of sums.

a. Thing
b. Binomial Theorem0
c. Undefined
d. Undefined

71. In mathematics, a _____ is a constant multiplicative factor of a certain object. The object can be such things as a variable, a vector, a function, etc. For example, the _____ of $9x^2$ is 9.

a. Thing
b. Coefficient0
c. Undefined
d. Undefined

72. In elementary algebra, a _____ is a polynomial with two terms: the sum of two monomials. It is the simplest kind of polynomial except for a monomial.

a. Thing
b. Binomial0
c. Undefined
d. Undefined

73. A _____ is a symbolic representation denoting a quantity or expression. It often represents an "unknown" quantity that has the potential to change.

a. Variable0
b. Thing
c. Undefined
d. Undefined

74. In mathematics, an _____ is any of the arguments, i.e. "inputs", to a function. Thus if we have a function f(x), then x is a _____.

a. Thing
b. Independent variable0
c. Undefined
d. Undefined

75. In a function the _____, is the variable which is the value, i.e. the "output", of the function.

a. Thing
b. Dependent variable0
c. Undefined
d. Undefined

76. Mathematical _____ is used to represent ideas.

a. Notation0
b. Thing
c. Undefined
d. Undefined

Chapter 4. DIFFERENTIATION

77. _____ was a German mathematician and philosopher. He invented calculus independently of Newton, and his notation is the one in general use since.
   a. Person
   b. Leibniz0
   c. Undefined
   d. Undefined

78. _____ named in honor of the 17th century German philosopher and mathematician Gottfried Wilhelm Leibniz, was originally the use of expressions such as dx and dy and to represent "infinitely small" or infinitesimal increments of quantities x and y, just as Äx and Äy represent finite increments of x and y respectively.
   a. Leibniz notation0
   b. Thing
   c. Undefined
   d. Undefined

79. In mathematics, _____ is an elementary arithmetic operation. When one of the numbers is a whole number, _____ is the repeated sum of the other number.
   a. Multiplication0
   b. Thing
   c. Undefined
   d. Undefined

80. In mathematics, a _____ number is a number which can be expressed as a ratio of two integers. Non-integer _____ numbers (commonly called fractions) are usually written as the vulgar fraction a / b, where b is not zero.
   a. Rational0
   b. Thing
   c. Undefined
   d. Undefined

81. In mathematics, a _____ is any function which can be written as the ratio of two polynomial functions.
   a. Thing
   b. Rational function0
   c. Undefined
   d. Undefined

82. In geometry, two lines or planes if one falls on the other in such a way as to create congruent adjacent angles. The term may be used as a noun or adjective. Thus, referring to Figure 1, the line AB is the _____ to CD through the point B.
   a. Thing
   b. Perpendicular0
   c. Undefined
   d. Undefined

83. _____ is a notation for writing numbers that is often used by scientists and mathematicians to make it easier to write large and small numbers.
   a. Thing
   b. Scientific notation0
   c. Undefined
   d. Undefined

84. The _____ is a method of finding the derivative of a function that is the quotient of two other functions for which derivatives exist.
   a. Quotient rule0
   b. Thing
   c. Undefined
   d. Undefined

85. In plane geometry, a _____ is a polygon with four equal sides, four right angles, and parallel opposite sides. In algebra, the _____ of a number is that number multiplied by itself.
   a. Square0
   b. Thing
   c. Undefined
   d. Undefined

86. _____ is a mathematical operation, written a^n, involving two numbers, the base a and the exponent n.

Chapter 4. DIFFERENTIATION

    a. Thing
    c. Undefined
    b. Exponentiating0
    d. Undefined

87. _____ is a mathematical operation, written a^n, involving two numbers, the base a and the exponent n.
    a. Exponentiation0
    b. Thing
    c. Undefined
    d. Undefined

88. In mathematics, a _____ is a type of conic section defined as the intersection between a right circular conical surface and a plane which cuts through both halves of the cone.
    a. Thing
    b. Hyperbola0
    c. Undefined
    d. Undefined

89. A _____ is an abstract model that uses mathematical language to describe the behavior of a system. Eykhoff defined a _____ as 'a representation of the essential aspects of an existing system which presents knowledge of that system in usable form'.
    a. Mathematical model0
    b. Thing
    c. Undefined
    d. Undefined

90. _____ is the chance that something is likely to happen or be the case.
    a. Probability0
    b. Thing
    c. Undefined
    d. Undefined

91. _____ is a special mathematical relationship between two quantities. Two quantities are called proportional if they vary in such a way that one of the quantities is a constant multiple of the other, or equivalently if they have a constant ratio.
    a. Proportionality0
    b. Thing
    c. Undefined
    d. Undefined

92. A _____ number is a positive integer which has a positive divisor other than one or itself.
    a. Thing
    b. Composite0
    c. Undefined
    d. Undefined

93. A _____, formed by the composition of one function on another, represents the application of the former to the result of the application of the latter to the argument of the composite.
    a. Thing
    b. Composite function0
    c. Undefined
    d. Undefined

94. In calculus, the _____ is a formula for the derivative of the composite of two functions.
    a. Chain rule0
    b. Concept
    c. Undefined
    d. Undefined

95. Deductive _____ is the kind of _____ in which the conclusion is necessitated by, or reached from, previously known facts (the premises).
    a. Thing
    b. Reasoning0
    c. Undefined
    d. Undefined

96. _____ is to give an equation R(x,y) = S(x,y) that at least in part has the same graph as y = f(x).
   a. Implicit differentiation0
   b. Thing
   c. Undefined
   d. Undefined

97. In mathematics, an _____ is a generalization for the concept of a function in which the dependent variable may not be given explicitly in terms of the independent variable.
   a. Thing
   b. Implicit function0
   c. Undefined
   d. Undefined

98. In mathematics, the multiplicative inverse of a number x, denoted $1/x$ or x^{-1}, is the number which, when multiplied by x, yields 1. The multiplicative inverse of x is also called the _____ of x.
   a. Reciprocal0
   b. Thing
   c. Undefined
   d. Undefined

99. The _____ of a solid object is the three-dimensional concept of how much space it occupies, often quantified numerically.
   a. Thing
   b. Volume0
   c. Undefined
   d. Undefined

100. _____, Greek for "knowledge of nature," is the branch of science concerned with the discovery and characterization of universal laws which govern matter, energy, space, and time.
   a. Physics0
   b. Thing
   c. Undefined
   d. Undefined

101. _____ is a physical property of a system that underlies the common notions of hot and cold; something that is hotter has the greater _____.
   a. Thing
   b. Temperature0
   c. Undefined
   d. Undefined

102. In Euclidean geometry, a uniform _____ is a linear transformation that enlargers or diminishes objects, and whose _____ factor is the same in all directions. This is also called homothethy.
   a. Scale0
   b. Thing
   c. Undefined
   d. Undefined

103. In differential calculus, _____ problems involve finding the rate at which a quantity is changing by relating that quantity to other quantities whose rates of change are known.
   a. Related rates0
   b. Thing
   c. Undefined
   d. Undefined

104. In classical geometry, a _____ of a circle or sphere is any line segment from its center to its boundary. By extension, the _____ of a circle or sphere is the length of any such segment. The _____ is half the diameter. In science and engineering the term _____ of curvature is commonly used as a synonym for _____.
   a. Thing
   b. Radius0
   c. Undefined
   d. Undefined

Chapter 4. DIFFERENTIATION

105. In mathematics, a _____ is the set of all points in three-dimensional space (R^3) which are at distance r from a fixed point of that space, where r is a positive real number called the radius of the _____. The fixed point is called the center or centre, and is not part of the _____ itself.
   a. Sphere0
   b. Thing
   c. Undefined
   d. Undefined

106. In business, particularly accounting, a _____ is the time intervals that the accounts, statement, payments, or other calculations cover.
   a. Period0
   b. Thing
   c. Undefined
   d. Undefined

107. In mathematics, there are several meanings of _____ depending on the subject.
   a. Degree0
   b. Thing
   c. Undefined
   d. Undefined

108. _____ is defined as the rate of change or derivative with respect to time of velocity.
   a. Acceleration0
   b. Thing
   c. Undefined
   d. Undefined

109. In Euclidean geometry, a _____ is the set of all points in a plane at a fixed distance, called the radius, from a given point, the center.
   a. Circle0
   b. Thing
   c. Undefined
   d. Undefined

110. In mathematics, an _____ .
   a. Ellipse0
   b. Thing
   c. Undefined
   d. Undefined

111. A _____ is a symbol or group of symbols, or a word in a natural language that represents a number.
   a. Thing
   b. Numeral0
   c. Undefined
   d. Undefined

112. In mathematics, the _____ of Bernoulli is an eight-shaped algebraic curve described by a Cartesian equation
   a. Thing
   b. Lemniscate0
   c. Undefined
   d. Undefined

113. In geometry, a _____ is defined as a quadrilateral where all four of its angles are right angles.
   a. Thing
   b. Rectangle0
   c. Undefined
   d. Undefined

114. _____ is the estimation of a physical quantity such as distance, energy, temperature, or time.
   a. Measurement0
   b. Thing
   c. Undefined
   d. Undefined

115. Initial objects are also called _____, and terminal objects are also called final.

Chapter 4. DIFFERENTIATION

    a. Coterminal0   b. Thing
    c. Undefined   d. Undefined

116. In mathematics, the _____ functions are functions of an angle; they are important when studying triangles and modeling periodic phenomena, among many other applications.
    a. Trigonometric0   b. Thing
    c. Undefined   d. Undefined

117. The _____ are functions of an angle; they are important when studying triangles and modeling periodic phenomena, among many other applications.
    a. Trigonometric functions0   b. Thing
    c. Undefined   d. Undefined

118. _____ is a trigonemtric function that is important when studying triangles and modeling periodic phenomena, among other applications.
    a. Sine0   b. Thing
    c. Undefined   d. Undefined

119. The _____ of an angle is the ratio of the length of the adjacent side to the length of the hypotenuse.
    a. Concept   b. Cosine0
    c. Undefined   d. Undefined

120. In mathematics, a _____ of a positive integer n is a way of writing n as a sum of positive integers.
    a. Thing   b. Composition0
    c. Undefined   d. Undefined

121. In mathematics, _____ growth occurs when the growth rate of a function is always proportional to the function's current size.
    a. Thing   b. Exponential0
    c. Undefined   d. Undefined

122. _____ is one of the most important functions in mathematics. A function commonly used to study growth and decay
    a. Exponential function0   b. Thing
    c. Undefined   d. Undefined

123. _____ was a French lawyer and a mathematician who is given credit for early developments that led to modern calculus. In particular, he is recognized for his discovery of an original method of finding the greatest and the smallest ordinates of curved lines, which is analogous to that of the then unknown differential calculus.
    a. Pierre de Fermat0   b. Person
    c. Undefined   d. Undefined

124. In geometry, a line _____ is a part of a line that is bounded by two end points, and contains every point on the line between its end points.

Chapter 4. DIFFERENTIATION

    a. Concept
    c. Undefined
    b. Segment0
    d. Undefined

125. A _____ is a part of a line that is bounded by two end points, and contains every point on the line between its end points.
    a. Thing
    b. Line segment0
    c. Undefined
    d. Undefined

126. Sir Isaac _____, was an English physicist, mathematician, astronomer, natural philosopher, and alchemist, regarded by many as the greatest figure in the history of science
    a. Person
    b. Newton0
    c. Undefined
    d. Undefined

127. In mathematics, two quantities are called _____ if they vary in such a way that one of the quantities is a constant multiple of the other, or equivalently if they have a constant ratio.
    a. Proportional0
    b. Thing
    c. Undefined
    d. Undefined

128. In mathematics, the _____ of a function is the set of all "output" values produced by that function. Given a function $f : A \to B$, the _____ of f, is defined to be the set $\{x \in B : x = f(a) \text{ for some } a \in A\}$.
    a. Thing
    b. Range0
    c. Undefined
    d. Undefined

129. _____ is a kind of property which exists as magnitude or multitude. It is among the basic classes of things along with quality, substance, change, and relation.
    a. Amount0
    b. Thing
    c. Undefined
    d. Undefined

130. _____ was an Austrian-born biologist known as one of the founders of general systems theory.
    a. Person
    b. Von Bertalanffy0
    c. Undefined
    d. Undefined

131. _____ element of an element x with respect to a binary operation * with identity element e is an element y such that x * y = y * x = e. In particular,
    a. Thing
    b. Inverse0
    c. Undefined
    d. Undefined

132. An _____ is a function which does the reverse of a given function.
    a. Inverse function0
    b. Thing
    c. Undefined
    d. Undefined

133. _____ is a test used to determine if a function is injective, surjective or bijective.
    a. Horizontal line test0
    b. Thing
    c. Undefined
    d. Undefined

134. _____ is a branch of mathematics concerning the study of structure, relation and quantity.

Chapter 4. DIFFERENTIATION

a. Concept
b. Algebra0
c. Undefined
d. Undefined

135. In mathematics, a _____ of a number x is the exponent y of the power by such that $x = b^y$. The value used for the base b must be neither 0 nor 1, nor a root of 1 in the case of the extension to complex numbers, and is typically 10, e, or 2.
   a. Logarithm0
   b. Thing
   c. Undefined
   d. Undefined

136. In mathematics, a _____ may be described informally as a number that can be given by an infinite decimal representation.
   a. Thing
   b. Real number0
   c. Undefined
   d. Undefined

137. In mathematics and its applications, _____ refers to finding the linear approximation to a function at a given point.
   a. Thing
   b. Linearization0
   c. Undefined
   d. Undefined

138. _____ is an approximation of a general function using a linear function more precisely, an affine function.
   a. Thing
   b. Linear approximation0
   c. Undefined
   d. Undefined

139. _____ is a synonym for information.
   a. Data0
   b. Thing
   c. Undefined
   d. Undefined

140. In geometry, a _____ (Greek words diairo = divide and metro = measure) of a circle is any straight line segment that passes through the centre and whose endpoints are on the circular boundary, or, in more modern usage, the length of such a line segment. When using the word in the more modern sense, one speaks of the _____ rather than a _____, because all diameters of a circle have the same length. This length is twice the radius. The _____ of a circle is also the longest chord that the circle has.
   a. Diameter0
   b. Thing
   c. Undefined
   d. Undefined

141. _____ comes from the Latin word linearis, which means created by lines.
   a. Linearity0
   b. Thing
   c. Undefined
   d. Undefined

142. A _____ is a deliberate process for transforming one or more inputs into one or more results.
   a. Thing
   b. Calculation0
   c. Undefined
   d. Undefined

143. _____ is the property of a physical object that quantifies the amount of matter and energy it is equivalent to.
   a. Thing
   b. Mass0
   c. Undefined
   d. Undefined

Chapter 4. DIFFERENTIATION

144. _____ is an adjective usually refering to being in the centre.
   a. Thing
   b. Central0
   c. Undefined
   d. Undefined

145. An _____ is a straight line around which a geometric figure can be rotated.
   a. Axis0
   b. Thing
   c. Undefined
   d. Undefined

146. In mathematics, the _____ of a coordinate system is the point where the axes of the system intersect.
   a. Origin0
   b. Thing
   c. Undefined
   d. Undefined

147. A _____ is a unit of length, usually used to measure distance, in a number of different systems, including Imperial units, United States customary units and Norwegian/Swedish mil. Its size can vary from system to system, but in each is between 1 and 10 kilometers. In contemporary English contexts _____ refers to either:
   a. Thing
   b. Mile0
   c. Undefined
   d. Undefined

Chapter 5. APPLICATIONS OF DIFFERENTIATION

1. in mathematics, maxima and minima, known collectively as _____, are the largest value maximum or smallest value minimum, that a function takes in a point either within a given neighborhood or on the function domain in its entirety global extremum.
   - a. Extrema0
   - b. Thing
   - c. Undefined
   - d. Undefined

2. The mathematical concept of a _____ expresses the intuitive idea of deterministic dependence between two quantities, one of which is viewed as primary and the other as secondary. A _____ then is a way to associate a unique output for each input of a specified type, for example, a real number or an element of a given set.
   - a. Function0
   - b. Thing
   - c. Undefined
   - d. Undefined

3. The _____, the average in everyday English, which is also called the arithmetic _____ (and is distinguished from the geometric _____ or harmonic _____). The average is also called the sample _____. The expected value of a random variable, which is also called the population _____.
   - a. Mean0
   - b. Thing
   - c. Undefined
   - d. Undefined

4. In mathematics, a _____ is a statement that can be proved on the basis of explicitly stated or previously agreed assumptions.
   - a. Theorem0
   - b. Thing
   - c. Undefined
   - d. Undefined

5. The term _____ refers to the largest and the smallest element of a set.
   - a. Extreme value0
   - b. Thing
   - c. Undefined
   - d. Undefined

6. _____ is the study of terms and their use — of words and compound words that are used in specific contexts.
   - a. Terminology0
   - b. Thing
   - c. Undefined
   - d. Undefined

7. A _____ function is a function for which, intuitively, small changes in the input result in small changes in the output.
   - a. Event
   - b. Continuous0
   - c. Undefined
   - d. Undefined

8. _____ is a free computer algebra system based on a 1982 version of Macsyma
   - a. Thing
   - b. Maxima0
   - c. Undefined
   - d. Undefined

9. In elementary algebra, an _____ is a set that contains every real number between two indicated numbers and may contain the two numbers themselves.
   - a. Interval0
   - b. Thing
   - c. Undefined
   - d. Undefined

10. In mathematics, maxima and _____, known collectively as extrema, are points in the domain of a function at which the function takes a largest value .

Chapter 5. APPLICATIONS OF DIFFERENTIATION

a. Minima0
b. Thing
c. Undefined
d. Undefined

11. In geometry, an _____ is a point at which a line segment or ray terminates.
   a. Endpoint0
   b. Thing
   c. Undefined
   d. Undefined

12. In mathematics, a _____ of a k-place relation $L \subseteq X_1 \times \ldots \times X_k$ is one of the sets X_j, $1 \le j \le k$. In the special case where k = 2 and $L \subseteq X_1 \times X_2$ is a function $L : X_1 \to X_2$, it is conventional to refer to X_1 as the _____ of the function and to refer to X_2 as the codomain of the function.
   a. Domain0
   b. Thing
   c. Undefined
   d. Undefined

13. A real-valued function f defined on the real line is said to have a _____ point at the point x∗, if there exists some ε > 0, such that f when x − x∗ < ε.
   a. Local maximum0
   b. Thing
   c. Undefined
   d. Undefined

14. In trigonometry, the _____ is a function defined as $\tan x = \sin x / \cos x$. The function is so-named because it can be defined as the length of a certain segment of a _____ (in the geometric sense) to the unit circle. In plane geometry, a line is _____ to a curve, at some point, if both line and curve pass through the point with the same direction.
   a. Tangent0
   b. Thing
   c. Undefined
   d. Undefined

15. _____ has two distinct but etymologically-related meanings: one in geometry and one in trigonometry.
   a. Thing
   b. Tangent line0
   c. Undefined
   d. Undefined

16. In mathematics, maxima and minima, known collectively as extrema, are the largest value maximum or smallest value minimum, that a function takes in a point either within a given neighborhood local _____ or on the function domain in its entirety global _____.
   a. Thing
   b. Extremum0
   c. Undefined
   d. Undefined

17. In astronomy, geography, geometry and related sciences and contexts, a plane is said to be _____ at a given point if it is locally perpendicular to the gradient of the gravity field, i.e., with the direction of the gravitational force at that point.
   a. Horizontal0
   b. Thing
   c. Undefined
   d. Undefined

18. The _____ is a measurement of how a function changes when the values of its inputs change.
   a. Thing
   b. Derivative0
   c. Undefined
   d. Undefined

19. Contraposition is the concept of how two qualities or statements relate to each other. In mathematics, in a statement "if P then Q" for any two propositions P and Q, then the converse is "if Q then P", the inverse is "if not P then not Q", and the _____ is "if not Q then not P".

a. Thing
b. Contrapositive0
c. Undefined
d. Undefined

20. The _____ integers are all the integers from zero on upwards.
a. Nonnegative0
b. Thing
c. Undefined
d. Undefined

21. _____ is a trigonometric function that is the reciprocal of cosine.
a. Secant0
b. Thing
c. Undefined
d. Undefined

22. _____ of a curve is a line that intersects two or more points on the curve.
a. Thing
b. Secant line0
c. Undefined
d. Undefined

23. A _____ is a negotiable instrument instructing a financial institution to pay a specific amount of a specific currency from a specific demand account held in the maker/depositor's name with that institution. Both the maker and payee may be natural persons or legal entities.
a. Check0
b. Thing
c. Undefined
d. Undefined

24. _____ is a mathematical subject that includes the study of limits, derivatives, integrals, and power series and constitutes a major part of modern university curriculum.
a. Calculus0
b. Thing
c. Undefined
d. Undefined

25. _____ of an object is its speed in a particular direction.
a. Thing
b. Velocity0
c. Undefined
d. Undefined

26. _____ is often used to describe the measurement of the steepness, incline, gradient, or grade of a straight line. The _____ is defined as the ratio of the "rise" divided by the "run" between two points on a line, or in other words, the ratio of the altitude change to the horizontal distance between any two points on the line.
a. Thing
b. Slope0
c. Undefined
d. Undefined

27. In mathematics, an _____, mean, or central tendency of a data set refers to a measure of the "middle" or "expected" value of the data set.
a. Average0
b. Concept
c. Undefined
d. Undefined

28. The metre (or _____, see spelling differences) is a measure of length. It is the basic unit of length in the metric system and in the International System of Units (SI), used around the world for general and scientific purposes.
a. Concept
b. Meter0
c. Undefined
d. Undefined

Chapter 5. APPLICATIONS OF DIFFERENTIATION

29. An _____ is a combination of numbers, operators, grouping symbols and/or free variables and bound variables arranged in a meaningful way which can be evaluated..
   a. Expression0
   b. Thing
   c. Undefined
   d. Undefined

30. In a mathematical proof or a syllogism, a _____ is a statement that is the logical consequence of preceding statements.
   a. Conclusion0
   b. Concept
   c. Undefined
   d. Undefined

31. In mathematics, a _____ is a demonstration that, assuming certain axioms, some statement is necessarily true.
   a. Proof0
   b. Thing
   c. Undefined
   d. Undefined

32. In mathematics and the mathematical sciences, a _____ is a fixed, but possibly unspecified, value. This is in contrast to a variable, which is not fixed.
   a. Constant0
   b. Thing
   c. Undefined
   d. Undefined

33. _____ is a function whose values do not vary and thus are constant.
   a. Thing
   b. Constant function0
   c. Undefined
   d. Undefined

34. A _____ is a mathematical statement which follows easily from a previously proven statement, typically a mathematical theorem.
   a. Corollary0
   b. Thing
   c. Undefined
   d. Undefined

35. _____ is a trigonemtric function that is important when studying triangles and modeling periodic phenomena, among other applications.
   a. Thing
   b. Sine0
   c. Undefined
   d. Undefined

36. An _____ is an equality that remains true regardless of the values of any variables that appear within it, to distinguish it from an equality which is true under more particular conditions.
   a. Identity0
   b. Thing
   c. Undefined
   d. Undefined

37. In mathematics, the _____ f is the collection of all ordered pairs . In particular, graph means the graphical representation of this collection, in the form of a curve or surface, together with axes, etc. Graphing on a Cartesian plane is sometimes referred to as curve sketching.
   a. Thing
   b. Graph of a function0
   c. Undefined
   d. Undefined

38. A _____ is a special kind of ratio, indicating a relationship between two measurements with different units, such as miles to gallons or cents to pounds.

Chapter 5. APPLICATIONS OF DIFFERENTIATION

a. Thing
b. Rate0
c. Undefined
d. Undefined

39. In sociology and biology a _____ is the collection of people or organisms of a particular species living in a given geographic area or space, usually measured by a census.
a. Thing
b. Population0
c. Undefined
d. Undefined

40. _____ is the middle point of a line segment.
a. Thing
b. Midpoint0
c. Undefined
d. Undefined

41. A _____ is traditionally an infinitesimally small change in a variable.
a. Differential0
b. Thing
c. Undefined
d. Undefined

42. A _____ is a mathematical equation for an unknown function of one or several variables which relates the values of the function itself and of its derivatives of various orders.
a. Thing
b. Differential equation0
c. Undefined
d. Undefined

43. The word _____ means curving in or hollowed inward.
a. Thing
b. Concavity0
c. Undefined
d. Undefined

44. In mathematics, functions between ordered sets are _____ or monotone, or even isotone if they preserve the given order.
a. Thing
b. Monotonic0
c. Undefined
d. Undefined

45. In mathematics, an _____ is a statement about the relative size or order of two objects.
a. Thing
b. Inequality0
c. Undefined
d. Undefined

46. Acid _____ ratio measures the ability of a company to use its near cash or quick assets to immediately extinguish its current liabilities.
a. Test0
b. Thing
c. Undefined
d. Undefined

47. _____ determines whether a given critical point of a function is a maximum, a minimum, or neither.
a. Thing
b. First Derivative Test0
c. Undefined
d. Undefined

48. In mathematics, a _____ is an expression that is constructed from one or more variables and constants, using only the operations of addition, subtraction, multiplication, and constant positive whole number exponents. is a _____. Note in particular that division by an expression containing a variable is not in general allowed in polynomials. [1]

Chapter 5. APPLICATIONS OF DIFFERENTIATION

    a. Thing
    c. Undefined
    b. Polynomial0
    d. Undefined

49. In calculus, the _____ is a formula for the derivative of the composite of two functions.
    a. Chain rule0
    c. Undefined
    b. Concept
    d. Undefined

50. In mathematics, a _____ is the end result of a division problem. It can also be expressed as the number of times the divisor divides into the dividend.
    a. Thing
    c. Undefined
    b. Quotient0
    d. Undefined

51. The _____ is a method of finding the derivative of a function that is the quotient of two other functions for which derivatives exist.
    a. Quotient rule0
    c. Undefined
    b. Thing
    d. Undefined

52. _____ are the basic objects of study in graph theory. Informally speaking, a graph is a set of objects called points, nodes, or vertices connected by links called lines or edges.
    a. Thing
    c. Undefined
    b. Graphs0
    d. Undefined

53. A _____ is a deliberate process for transforming one or more inputs into one or more results.
    a. Calculation0
    c. Undefined
    b. Thing
    d. Undefined

54. In mathematics, two quantities are called _____ if they vary in such a way that one of the quantities is a constant multiple of the other, or equivalently if they have a constant ratio.
    a. Proportional0
    c. Undefined
    b. Thing
    d. Undefined

55. The word _____ comes from the Latin word linearis, which means created by lines.
    a. Linear0
    c. Undefined
    b. Thing
    d. Undefined

56. A _____ is a first degree polynomial mathematical function of the form: $f(x) = mx + b$ where m and b are real constants and x is a real variable.
    a. Thing
    c. Undefined
    b. Linear function0
    d. Undefined

57. A _____ is a function for which, intuitively, small changes in the input result in small changes in the output.
    a. Continuous function0
    c. Undefined
    b. Event
    d. Undefined

Chapter 5. APPLICATIONS OF DIFFERENTIATION

58. In mathematics, the additive inverse, or _____ of a number n is the number that, when added to n, yields zero. The additive inverse of n is denoted −n. For example, 7 is −7, because 7 + (−7) = 0, and the additive inverse of −0.3 is 0.3, because −0.3 + 0.3 = 0.
    a. Opposite0
    b. Thing
    c. Undefined
    d. Undefined

59. The _____ implies that on any great circle around the world, the temperature, pressure, elevation, carbon dioxide concentration, or anything else that varies continuously, there will always exist two antipodal points that share the same value for that variable.
    a. Intermediate Value Theorem0
    b. Thing
    c. Undefined
    d. Undefined

60. In mathematics, the _____ of a number n is the number that, when added to n, yields zero. The _____ of n is denoted −n. For example, 7 is −7, because 7 + (−7) = 0, and the _____ of −0.3 is 0.3, because −0.3 + 0.3 = 0.
    a. Thing
    b. Additive inverse0
    c. Undefined
    d. Undefined

61. _____ is a kind of property which exists as magnitude or multitude. It is among the basic classes of things along with quality, substance, change, and relation.
    a. Amount0
    b. Thing
    c. Undefined
    d. Undefined

62. _____ is mass m per unit volume V.
    a. Thing
    b. Density0
    c. Undefined
    d. Undefined

63. _____ is the chance that something is likely to happen or be the case.
    a. Probability0
    b. Thing
    c. Undefined
    d. Undefined

64. _____ or investing is a term with several closely-related meanings in business management, finance and economics, related to saving or deferring consumption.
    a. Thing
    b. Investment0
    c. Undefined
    d. Undefined

65. In mathematics, the concept of a _____ tries to capture the intuitive idea of a geometrical one-dimensional and continuous object. A simple example is the circle.
    a. Curve0
    b. Thing
    c. Undefined
    d. Undefined

66. In economics, economic _____ is simply a state of the world where economic forces are balanced and in the absence of external influences the values of economic variables will not change.
    a. Thing
    b. Equilibrium0
    c. Undefined
    d. Undefined

67. A _____ is the quantity that defines certain relatively constant characteristics of systems or functions..

Chapter 5. APPLICATIONS OF DIFFERENTIATION

a. Thing
b. Parameter0
c. Undefined
d. Undefined

68. _____ is to give an equation R(x,y) = S(x,y) that at least in part has the same graph as y = f(x).
a. Implicit differentiation0
b. Thing
c. Undefined
d. Undefined

69. _____, a field in mathematics, is the study of how functions change when their inputs change. The primary object of study in _____ is the derivative.
a. Thing
b. Differential calculus0
c. Undefined
d. Undefined

70. _____ is the logarithm to the base e, where e is an irrational constant approximately equal to 2.718281828459.
a. Thing
b. Natural logarithm0
c. Undefined
d. Undefined

71. In mathematics, a _____ of a number x is the exponent y of the power by such that $x = b^y$. The value used for the base b must be neither 0 nor 1, nor a root of 1 in the case of the extension to complex numbers, and is typically 10, e, or 2.
a. Logarithm0
b. Thing
c. Undefined
d. Undefined

72. _____ is the estimation of a physical quantity such as distance, energy, temperature, or time.
a. Measurement0
b. Thing
c. Undefined
d. Undefined

73. In geometry, a _____ (Greek words diairo = divide and metro = measure) of a circle is any straight line segment that passes through the centre and whose endpoints are on the circular boundary, or, in more modern usage, the length of such a line segment. When using the word In the more modern sense, one speaks of the _____ rather than a _____, because all diameters of a circle have the same length. This length is twice the radius. The _____ of a circle is also the longest chord that the circle has.
a. Thing
b. Diameter0
c. Undefined
d. Undefined

74. A _____ is a function that assigns a number to subsets of a given set.
a. Thing
b. Measure0
c. Undefined
d. Undefined

75. _____ is a a point on a curve at which the tangent crosses the curve itself.
a. Inflection point0
b. Thing
c. Undefined
d. Undefined

76. A _____ is a symbolic representation denoting a quantity or expression. It often represents an "unknown" quantity that has the potential to change.
a. Variable0
b. Thing
c. Undefined
d. Undefined

Chapter 5. APPLICATIONS OF DIFFERENTIATION

77. In mathematics, a _____ may be described informally as a number that can be given by an infinite decimal representation.
   a. Real number0
   b. Thing
   c. Undefined
   d. Undefined

78. _____ is a point on the domain of a function
   a. Thing
   b. Critical point0
   c. Undefined
   d. Undefined

79. The plus and _____ signs are mathematical symbols used to represent the notions of positive and negative as well as the operations of addition and subtraction.
   a. Minus0
   b. Thing
   c. Undefined
   d. Undefined

80. In mathematics, a _____ is the result of multiplying, or an expression that identifies factors to be multiplied.
   a. Product0
   b. Thing
   c. Undefined
   d. Undefined

81. The _____ governs the differentiation of products of differentiable functions.
   a. Thing
   b. Product rule0
   c. Undefined
   d. Undefined

82. An _____ is a straight line or curve A to which another curve B approaches closer and closer as one moves along it. As one moves along B, the space between it and the _____ A becomes smaller and smaller, and can in fact be made as small as one could wish by going far enough along. A curve may or may not touch or cross its _____. In fact, the curve may intersect the _____ an infinite number of times.
   a. Thing
   b. Asymptote0
   c. Undefined
   d. Undefined

83. _____ is a straight line or curve A to which another curve B the one being studied approaches closer and closer as one moves along it.
   a. Thing
   b. Vertical asymptote0
   c. Undefined
   d. Undefined

84. In geometry, an _____ angle is an angle that is not a 90 degree angle, or an angle that is divisible by 90: 180, 270, 360/0
   a. Oblique0
   b. Thing
   c. Undefined
   d. Undefined

85. A _____ is a numeral used to indicate a count. The most common use of the word today is to name the part of a fraction that tells the number or count of equal parts.
   a. Thing
   b. Numerator0
   c. Undefined
   d. Undefined

86. In mathematics, a _____ number is a number which can be expressed as a ratio of two integers. Non-integer _____ numbers (commonly called fractions) are usually written as the vulgar fraction a / b, where b is not zero.

Chapter 5. APPLICATIONS OF DIFFERENTIATION

a. Thing
b. Rational0
c. Undefined
d. Undefined

87. In mathematics, a _____ is any function which can be written as the ratio of two polynomial functions.
a. Rational function0
b. Thing
c. Undefined
d. Undefined

88. In mathematics, there are several meanings of _____ depending on the subject.
a. Thing
b. Degree0
c. Undefined
d. Undefined

89. A _____ is the part of a fraction that tells how many equal parts make up a whole, and which is used in the name of the fraction: "halves", "thirds", "fourths" or "quarters", "fifths" and so on.
a. Denominator0
b. Concept
c. Undefined
d. Undefined

90. In arithmetic, _____ is a procedure for calculating the division of one integer, called the dividend, by another integer called the divisor, to produce a result called the quotient.
a. Thing
b. Long division0
c. Undefined
d. Undefined

91. In mathematics, defined and _____ are used to explain whether or not expressions have meaningful, sensible, and unambiguous values.
a. Undefined0
b. Thing
c. Undefined
d. Undefined

92. A _____ is a set of numbers that designate location in a given reference system, such as x,y in a planar _____ system or an x,y,z in a three-dimensional _____ system.
a. Coordinate0
b. Thing
c. Undefined
d. Undefined

93. _____ are points in the domain of a function at which the function takes a largest value or smallest value, either within a given neighborhood or on the function domain in its entirety.
a. Maxima and minima0
b. Thing
c. Undefined
d. Undefined

94. _____ Any process by which a specified characteristic usually amplitude of the output of a device is prevented from exceeding a predetermined value.
a. Limiting0
b. Thing
c. Undefined
d. Undefined

95. In mathematics, an inequality is a statement about the relative size or order of two objects. For example 14 > 10, or 14 is _____ 10.
a. Greater than0
b. Thing
c. Undefined
d. Undefined

Chapter 5. APPLICATIONS OF DIFFERENTIATION

96. In computer science, an _____ is the problem of finding the best solution from all feasible solutions.
   a. Thing
   b. Optimization problem0
   c. Undefined
   d. Undefined

97. When _____ symmetry one can determine whether or not an object is symmetric with respect to a given mathematical operation, if, when applied to the object, this operation does not change the object or its appearance.
   a. Thing
   b. Investigating0
   c. Undefined
   d. Undefined

98. The _____ of measurement are a globally standardized and modernized form of the metric system.
   a. Thing
   b. Units0
   c. Undefined
   d. Undefined

99. _____ is the distance around a given two-dimensional object. As a general rule, the _____ of a polygon can always be calculated by adding all the length of the sides together. So, the formula for triangles is P = a + b + c, where a, b and c stand for each side of it. For quadrilaterals the equation is P = a + b + c + d. For equilateral polygons, P = na, where n is the number of sides and a is the side length.
   a. Perimeter0
   b. Thing
   c. Undefined
   d. Undefined

100. In geometry, a _____ is defined as a quadrilateral where all four of its angles are right angles.
   a. Rectangle0
   b. Thing
   c. Undefined
   d. Undefined

101. In plane geometry, a _____ is a polygon with four equal sides, four right angles, and parallel opposite sides. In algebra, the _____ of a number is that number multiplied by itself.
   a. Square0
   b. Thing
   c. Undefined
   d. Undefined

102. In mathematics, a _____ is a quadric surface, with the following equation in Cartesian coordinates: $(x/_a)^2 + (y/_b)^2 = 1$.
   a. Thing
   b. Cylinder0
   c. Undefined
   d. Undefined

103. The _____ of a solid object is the three-dimensional concept of how much space it occupies, often quantified numerically.
   a. Thing
   b. Volume0
   c. Undefined
   d. Undefined

104. In classical geometry, a _____ of a circle or sphere is any line segment from its center to its boundary. By extension, the _____ of a circle or sphere is the length of any such segment. The _____ is half the diameter. In science and engineering the term _____ of curvature is commonly used as a synonym for _____.
   a. Radius0
   b. Thing
   c. Undefined
   d. Undefined

Chapter 5. APPLICATIONS OF DIFFERENTIATION

105. In topology, the _____ are subsets S of a topological space X is the set of points which can be approached both from S and from the outside of S.
   a. Thing
   b. Boundaries0
   c. Undefined
   d. Undefined

106. In mathematics, a _____ is a condition that a solution to an optimization problem must satisfy in order to be acceptable.
   a. Thing
   b. Constraint0
   c. Undefined
   d. Undefined

107. In mathematics, the word _____ is used informally to refer to certain distinct bodies of knowledge about mathematics.
   a. Thing
   b. Theoretical0
   c. Undefined
   d. Undefined

108. In mathematical analysis and related areas of mathematics, a set is called _____, if it is, in a certain sense, of finite size.
   a. Bounded0
   b. Thing
   c. Undefined
   d. Undefined

109. A _____ is one of the basic shapes of geometry: a polygon with three vertices and three sides which are straight line segments.
   a. Triangle0
   b. Thing
   c. Undefined
   d. Undefined

110. The _____ of a right triangle is the triangle's longest side; the side opposite the right angle.
   a. Hypotenuse0
   b. Thing
   c. Undefined
   d. Undefined

111. _____ has one 90° internal angle a right angle.
   a. Thing
   b. Right triangle0
   c. Undefined
   d. Undefined

112. In mathematics, the _____ of a coordinate system is the point where the axes of the system intersect.
   a. Thing
   b. Origin0
   c. Undefined
   d. Undefined

113. In Euclidean geometry, an _____ is a closed segment of a differentiable curve in the two-dimensional plane; for example, a circular _____ is a segment of a circle.
   a. Concept
   b. Arc0
   c. Undefined
   d. Undefined

114. A circular _____ or circle _____ also known as a pie piece is the portion of a circle enclosed by two radii and an arc.

Chapter 5. APPLICATIONS OF DIFFERENTIATION

a. Thing
b. Sector0
c. Undefined
d. Undefined

115. The _____ is a unit of plane angle. It is represented by the symbol "rad" or, more rarely, by the superscript c (for "circular measure"). For example, an angle of 1.2 radians would be written "1.2 rad" or "1.2c" (second symbol can produce confusion with centigrads).
a. Thing
b. Radian0
c. Undefined
d. Undefined

116. In combinatorial mathematics, a _____ is an un-ordered collection of unique elements.
a. Concept
b. Combination0
c. Undefined
d. Undefined

117. In statistics the _____ of an event i is the number n_i of times the event occurred in the experiment or the study. These frequencies are often graphically represented in histograms.
a. Frequency0
b. Concept
c. Undefined
d. Undefined

118. _____ (Basel, July 27, 1667 - January 1, 1748) was a Swiss mathematician.
a. Johann Bernoulli0
b. Person
c. Undefined
d. Undefined

119. _____ is a form of periodic payment from an employer to an employee, which is specified in an employment contract.
a. Gross pay0
b. Thing
c. Undefined
d. Undefined

120. A _____ is a form of periodic payment from an employer to an employee, which is specified in an employment contract.
a. Thing
b. Salary0
c. Undefined
d. Undefined

121. _____ is the state of being greater than any finite number, however large.
a. Infinity0
b. Thing
c. Undefined
d. Undefined

122. _____ is an approximation of a general function using a linear function more precisely, an affine function.
a. Linear approximation0
b. Thing
c. Undefined
d. Undefined

123. A _____ is a quantity that denotes the proportional amount or magnitude of one quantity relative to another.
a. Ratio0
b. Thing
c. Undefined
d. Undefined

124. _____ is the state of being greater than any finite real or natural number, however large.

Chapter 5. APPLICATIONS OF DIFFERENTIATION

a. Infinite0
b. Thing
c. Undefined
d. Undefined

125. _____ has many meanings, most of which simply .
a. Power0
b. Thing
c. Undefined
d. Undefined

126. In mathematics, _____ growth occurs when the growth rate of a function is always proportional to the function's current size.
a. Thing
b. Exponential0
c. Undefined
d. Undefined

127. _____ is one of the most important functions in mathematics. A function commonly used to study growth and decay
a. Thing
b. Exponential function0
c. Undefined
d. Undefined

128. _____ is a method of defining functions in which the function being defined is applied within its own definition. The term is also used more generally to describe a process of repeating objects in a self-similar way.
a. Recursion0
b. Thing
c. Undefined
d. Undefined

129. In mathematics, _____ occurs when the growth rate of a function is always proportional to the function's current size.
a. Thing
b. Exponential growth0
c. Undefined
d. Undefined

130. The word _____ comes from the 15th Century Latin word discretus which means separate.
a. Thing
b. Discrete0
c. Undefined
d. Undefined

131. Initial objects are also called _____, and terminal objects are also called final.
a. Thing
b. Coterminal0
c. Undefined
d. Undefined

132. In mathematics, in the field of differential equations, an initial value problem is a differential equation together with specified value, called the _____, of the unknown function at a given point in the domain of the solution.
a. Thing
b. Initial condition0
c. Undefined
d. Undefined

133. An _____ is a straight line around which a geometric figure can be rotated.
a. Thing
b. Axis0
c. Undefined
d. Undefined

134. One of the three formats applicable to a quadratic function is the _____ which is defined as $f = ax^2 + bx + c$.

Chapter 5. APPLICATIONS OF DIFFERENTIATION

  a. General form0
  b. Thing
  c. Undefined
  d. Undefined

135. A _____ of a number is the product of that number with any integer.
  a. Multiple0
  b. Thing
  c. Undefined
  d. Undefined

136. In mathematics, the _____ of two sets A and B is the set that contains all elements of A that also belong to B (or equivalently, all elements of B that also belong to A), but no other elements.
  a. Thing
  b. Intersection0
  c. Undefined
  d. Undefined

137. In mathematics and its applications, _____ refers to finding the linear approximation to a function at a given point.
  a. Linearization0
  b. Thing
  c. Undefined
  d. Undefined

138. In mathematics, a _____ is an ordered list of objects. Like a set, it contains members, also called elements or terms, and the number of terms is called the length of the _____. Unlike a set, order matters, and the exact same elements can appear multiple times at different positions in the _____.
  a. Thing
  b. Sequence0
  c. Undefined
  d. Undefined

139. In mathematics, a _____ of a complex-valued function f is a member x of the domain of f such that f(x) vanishes at x, that is, x : f (x) = 0.
  a. Thing
  b. Root0
  c. Undefined
  d. Undefined

140. Sir Isaac _____, was an English physicist, mathematician, astronomer, natural philosopher, and alchemist, regarded by many as the greatest figure in the history of science
  a. Newton0
  b. Person
  c. Undefined
  d. Undefined

141. A _____ is 360° or 2∂ radians.
  a. Thing
  b. Turn0
  c. Undefined
  d. Undefined

142. An _____ of a function f is a function F whose derivative is equal to f, i.e., F' = f.
  a. Antiderivative0
  b. Thing
  c. Undefined
  d. Undefined

143. _____ is a differential equation together with specified value, called the initial condition, of the unknown function at a given point in the domain of the solution.
  a. Thing
  b. Initial value problem0
  c. Undefined
  d. Undefined

Chapter 5. APPLICATIONS OF DIFFERENTIATION

144. _____ is defined as the rate of change or derivative with respect to time of velocity.
 a. Thing
 b. Acceleration0
 c. Undefined
 d. Undefined

145. In mathematics a _____ is a function which defines a distance between elements of a set.
 a. Thing
 b. Metric0
 c. Undefined
 d. Undefined

146. In mathematics, the factorial of a non-negative integer n is the product of all positive integers less than or equal to n. This is written as n! and pronounced _____, or colloquially "n shriek", "n bang" or "n crit".
 a. Thing
 b. N factorial0
 c. Undefined
 d. Undefined

147. _____ of a non-negative integer n is the product of all positive integers less than or equal to n.
 a. Thing
 b. Factorial0
 c. Undefined
 d. Undefined

Chapter 6. INTEGRATION

1. A _____ is one of the basic shapes of geometry: a polygon with three vertices and three sides which are straight line segments.
   a. Triangle0
   b. Thing
   c. Undefined
   d. Undefined

2. _____ is the fee paid on borrowed money.
   a. Thing
   b. Interest0
   c. Undefined
   d. Undefined

3. In mathematics, the concept of a _____ tries to capture the intuitive idea of a geometrical one-dimensional and continuous object. A simple example is the circle.
   a. Thing
   b. Curve0
   c. Undefined
   d. Undefined

4. In mathematics, _____ are the intuitive idea of a geometrical one-dimensional and continuous object.
   a. Thing
   b. Curves0
   c. Undefined
   d. Undefined

5. In mathematical analysis and related areas of mathematics, a set is called _____, if it is, in a certain sense, of finite size.
   a. Bounded0
   b. Thing
   c. Undefined
   d. Undefined

6. In geometry, a _____ is defined as a quadrilateral where all four of its angles are right angles.
   a. Rectangle0
   b. Thing
   c. Undefined
   d. Undefined

7. A _____ is the result of the addition of a set of numbers. The numbers may be natural numbers, complex numbers, matrices, or still more complicated objects. An infinite _____ is a subtle procedure known as a series.
   a. Thing
   b. Sum0
   c. Undefined
   d. Undefined

8. The mathematical concept of a _____ expresses the intuitive idea of deterministic dependence between two quantities, one of which is viewed as primary and the other as secondary. A _____ then is a way to associate a unique output for each input of a specified type, for example, a real number or an element of a given set.
   a. Function0
   b. Thing
   c. Undefined
   d. Undefined

9. _____ is an extension of the concept of a sum.
   a. Definite integral0
   b. Thing
   c. Undefined
   d. Undefined

10. The _____ of a function is an extension of the concept of a sum, and are identified or found through the use of integration.
    a. Integral0
    b. Thing
    c. Undefined
    d. Undefined

Chapter 6. INTEGRATION

11. In elementary algebra, an _____ is a set that contains every real number between two indicated numbers and may contain the two numbers themselves.
    a. Thing
    b. Interval0
    c. Undefined
    d. Undefined

12. In geometry, an _____ is a point at which a line segment or ray terminates.
    a. Thing
    b. Endpoint0
    c. Undefined
    d. Undefined

13. A _____ is a number, figure, or indicator that appears below the normal line of type, typically used in a formula, mathematical expression, or description of a chemical compound.
    a. Subscript0
    b. Thing
    c. Undefined
    d. Undefined

14. Mathematical _____ is used to represent ideas.
    a. Notation0
    b. Thing
    c. Undefined
    d. Undefined

15. _____ is the eighteenth letter of the Greek alphabet.
    a. Sigma0
    b. Thing
    c. Undefined
    d. Undefined

16. _____ is used as the symbol for summation. Summation is the addition of a set of numbers; the result is their sum. The "numbers" to be summed may be natural numbers, complex numbers, matrices, or still more complicated objects. An infinite sum is a subtle procedure known as a series.
    a. Sigma notation0
    b. Thing
    c. Undefined
    d. Undefined

17. In mathematics, a _____ may be described informally as a number that can be given by an infinite decimal representation.
    a. Real number0
    b. Thing
    c. Undefined
    d. Undefined

18. In mathematics, a set is called _____ if there is a bijection between the set and some set of the form {1, 2, ..., n} where n is a natural number.
    a. Thing
    b. Finite0
    c. Undefined
    d. Undefined

19. The _____ are the only integral domain whose positive elements are well-ordered, and in which order is preserved by addition. Like the natural numbers, the _____ form a countably infinite set. The set of all _____ is usually denoted in mathematics by a boldface Z .
    a. Thing
    b. Integers0
    c. Undefined
    d. Undefined

20. Generally, a _____ is a splitting of something into parts.

a. Thing
b. Partition0
c. Undefined
d. Undefined

21. An _____ or member of a set is an object that when collected together make up the set.
   a. Thing
   b. Element0
   c. Undefined
   d. Undefined

22. In mathematics, a _____ is the result of multiplying, or an expression that identifies factors to be multiplied.
   a. Thing
   b. Product0
   c. Undefined
   d. Undefined

23. _____ is a method for approximating the values of integrals.
   a. Riemann sum0
   b. Thing
   c. Undefined
   d. Undefined

24. The _____, the average in everyday English, which is also called the arithmetic _____ (and is distinguished from the geometric _____ or harmonic _____). The average is also called the sample _____. The expected value of a random variable, which is also called the population _____.
   a. Thing
   b. Mean0
   c. Undefined
   d. Undefined

25. _____ is the middle point of a line segment.
   a. Midpoint0
   b. Thing
   c. Undefined
   d. Undefined

26. In mathematics, a _____ is an ordered list of objects. Like a set, it contains members, also called elements or terms, and the number of terms is called the length of the _____. Unlike a set, order matters, and the exact same elements can appear multiple times at different positions in the _____.
   a. Sequence0
   b. Thing
   c. Undefined
   d. Undefined

27. _____ is a function that extends the concept of an ordinary sum
   a. Integrand0
   b. Thing
   c. Undefined
   d. Undefined

28. A _____ is a symbolic representation denoting a quantity or expression. It often represents an "unknown" quantity that has the potential to change.
   a. Variable0
   b. Thing
   c. Undefined
   d. Undefined

29. In mathematics, an _____ is any of the arguments, i.e. "inputs", to a function. Thus if we have a function f(x), then x is a _____.
   a. Independent variable0
   b. Thing
   c. Undefined
   d. Undefined

Chapter 6. INTEGRATION

30. A _____ function is a function for which, intuitively, small changes in the input result in small changes in the output.
    a. Continuous0
    b. Event
    c. Undefined
    d. Undefined

31. In mathematics, a _____ is a statement that can be proved on the basis of explicitly stated or previously agreed assumptions.
    a. Thing
    b. Theorem0
    c. Undefined
    d. Undefined

32. _____ is the state of being greater than any finite number, however large.
    a. Infinity0
    b. Thing
    c. Undefined
    d. Undefined

33. A _____ defined function $f(x)$ of a real variable x is a function whose definition is given differently on disjoint subsets of its domain.
    a. Thing
    b. Piecewise0
    c. Undefined
    d. Undefined

34. In mathematics, the _____ is a conic section generated by the intersection of a right circular conical surface and a plane parallel to a generating straight line of that surface. It can also be defined as locus of points in a plane which are equidistant from a given point.
    a. Parabola0
    b. Thing
    c. Undefined
    d. Undefined

35. A _____ consists of one quarter of the coordinate plane.
    a. Quadrant0
    b. Thing
    c. Undefined
    d. Undefined

36. In geometry, the _____ of an object is a point in some sense in the middle of the object.
    a. Center0
    b. Thing
    c. Undefined
    d. Undefined

37. In Euclidean geometry, a _____ is the set of all points in a plane at a fixed distance, called the radius, from a given point, the center.
    a. Thing
    b. Circle0
    c. Undefined
    d. Undefined

38. In classical geometry, a _____ of a circle or sphere is any line segment from its center to its boundary. By extension, the _____ of a circle or sphere is the length of any such segment. The _____ is half the diameter. In science and engineering the term _____ of curvature is commonly used as a synonym for _____.
    a. Thing
    b. Radius0
    c. Undefined
    d. Undefined

39. _____ is a process of combining or accumulating. It may also refer to:

a. Thing
b. Integration0
c. Undefined
d. Undefined

40. In mathematics and the mathematical sciences, a _____ is a fixed, but possibly unspecified, value. This is in contrast to a variable, which is not fixed.
    a. Constant0
    b. Thing
    c. Undefined
    d. Undefined

41. In mathematics, a _____ is a demonstration that, assuming certain axioms, some statement is necessarily true.
    a. Thing
    b. Proof0
    c. Undefined
    d. Undefined

42. The _____ integers are all the integers from zero on upwards.
    a. Thing
    b. Nonnegative0
    c. Undefined
    d. Undefined

43. The _____ of an algebraic expression is the same equation, but without parentheses.
    a. Expanded form0
    b. Thing
    c. Undefined
    d. Undefined

44. An _____ is a combination of numbers, operators, grouping symbols and/or free variables and bound variables arranged in a meaningful way which can be evaluated..
    a. Thing
    b. Expression0
    c. Undefined
    d. Undefined

45. In mathematics, an _____ is a statement about the relative size or order of two objects.
    a. Thing
    b. Inequality0
    c. Undefined
    d. Undefined

46. _____ is the chance that something is likely to happen or be the case.
    a. Probability0
    b. Thing
    c. Undefined
    d. Undefined

47. A _____ is a special kind of ratio, indicating a relationship between two measurements with different units, such as miles to gallons or cents to pounds.
    a. Thing
    b. Rate0
    c. Undefined
    d. Undefined

48. A _____ is a function that assigns a number to subsets of a given set.
    a. Measure0
    b. Thing
    c. Undefined
    d. Undefined

49. _____ is a mathematical subject that includes the study of limits, derivatives, integrals, and power series and constitutes a major part of modern university curriculum.

Chapter 6. INTEGRATION

    a. Calculus0
    c. Undefined
    b. Thing
    d. Undefined

50. In number theory, the _____ of arithmetic (or unique factorization theorem) states that every natural number greater than 1 can be written as a unique product of prime numbers.
    a. Fundamental theorem0
    c. Undefined
    b. Concept
    d. Undefined

51. _____ of calculus is the statement that the two central operations of calculus, differentiation and integration, are inverse operations: if a continuous function is first integrated and then differentiated, the original function is retrieved.
    a. Fundamental Theorem of Calculus0
    c. Undefined
    b. Thing
    d. Undefined

52. A _____ is 360° or 2∂ radians.
    a. Turn0
    c. Undefined
    b. Thing
    d. Undefined

53. In trigonometry, the _____ is a function defined as $\tan x = \sin x / \cos x$. The function is so-named because it can be defined as the length of a certain segment of a _____ (in the geometric sense) to the unit circle. In plane geometry, a line is _____ to a curve, at some point, if both line and curve pass through the point with the same direction.
    a. Thing
    c. Undefined
    b. Tangent0
    d. Undefined

54. Sir Isaac _____, was an English physicist, mathematician, astronomer, natural philosopher, and alchemist, regarded by many as the greatest figure in the history of science
    a. Person
    c. Undefined
    b. Newton0
    d. Undefined

55. _____ was a German mathematician and philosopher. He invented calculus independently of Newton, and his notation is the one in general use since.
    a. Person
    c. Undefined
    b. Leibniz0
    d. Undefined

56. An _____ of a function f is a function F whose derivative is equal to f, i.e., F' = f.
    a. Thing
    c. Undefined
    b. Antiderivative0
    d. Undefined

57. An _____ is a straight line around which a geometric figure can be rotated.
    a. Axis0
    c. Undefined
    b. Thing
    d. Undefined

58. In astronomy, geography, geometry and related sciences and contexts, a plane is said to be _____ at a given point if it is locally perpendicular to the gradient of the gravity field, i.e., with the direction of the gravitational force at that point.
    a. Thing
    c. Undefined
    b. Horizontal0
    d. Undefined

Chapter 6. INTEGRATION

59. The _____ is a measurement of how a function changes when the values of its inputs change.
    a. Derivative0
    b. Thing
    c. Undefined
    d. Undefined

60. In mathematics, science including computer science, linguistics and engineering, an _____ is, generally speaking, an independent variable or input to a function.
    a. Thing
    b. Argument0
    c. Undefined
    d. Undefined

61. A _____ is the part of the dividend that is left over when the dividend is not evenly divisible by the divisor.
    a. Thing
    b. Remainder0
    c. Undefined
    d. Undefined

62. In calculus, the _____ is a formula for the derivative of the composite of two functions.
    a. Chain rule0
    b. Concept
    c. Undefined
    d. Undefined

63. The plus and _____ signs are mathematical symbols used to represent the notions of positive and negative as well as the operations of addition and subtraction.
    a. Thing
    b. Minus0
    c. Undefined
    d. Undefined

64. The _____ implies that on any great circle around the world, the temperature, pressure, elevation, carbon dioxide concentration, or anything else that varies continuously, there will always exist two antipodal points that share the same value for that variable.
    a. Thing
    b. Intermediate Value Theorem0
    c. Undefined
    d. Undefined

65. In mathematics, _____ growth occurs when the growth rate of a function is always proportional to the function's current size.
    a. Exponential0
    b. Thing
    c. Undefined
    d. Undefined

66. _____ is one of the most important functions in mathematics. A function commonly used to study growth and decay
    a. Thing
    b. Exponential function0
    c. Undefined
    d. Undefined

67. _____ element of an element x with respect to a binary operation * with identity element e is an element y such that x * y = y * x = e. In particular,
    a. Inverse0
    b. Thing
    c. Undefined
    d. Undefined

68. An _____ is a function which does the reverse of a given function.

Chapter 6. INTEGRATION

a. Inverse function0
b. Thing
c. Undefined
d. Undefined

69. A _____ is a negotiable instrument instructing a financial institution to pay a specific amount of a specific currency from a specific demand account held in the maker/depositor's name with that institution. Both the maker and payee may be natural persons or legal entities.
   a. Check0
   b. Thing
   c. Undefined
   d. Undefined

70. _____ is a straight line or curve A to which another curve B the one being studied approaches closer and closer as one moves along it.
   a. Vertical asymptote0
   b. Thing
   c. Undefined
   d. Undefined

71. An _____ is a straight line or curve A to which another curve B approaches closer and closer as one moves along it. As one moves along B, the space between it and the _____ A becomes smaller and smaller, and can in fact be made as small as one could wish by going far enough along. A curve may or may not touch or cross its _____. In fact, the curve may intersect the _____ an infinite number of times.
   a. Thing
   b. Asymptote0
   c. Undefined
   d. Undefined

72. In topology and related areas of mathematics a _____ or Moore-Smith sequence is a generalization of a sequence, intended to unify the various notions of limit and generalize them to arbitrary topological spaces.
   a. Net0
   b. Thing
   c. Undefined
   d. Undefined

73. The _____ of a solid object is the three-dimensional concept of how much space it occupies, often quantified numerically.
   a. Thing
   b. Volume0
   c. Undefined
   d. Undefined

74. In mathematics, an _____, mean, or central tendency of a data set refers to a measure of the "middle" or "expected" value of the data set.
   a. Average0
   b. Concept
   c. Undefined
   d. Undefined

75. An _____ is an increase, either of some fixed amount, for example added regularly, or of a variable amount.
   a. Increment0
   b. Thing
   c. Undefined
   d. Undefined

76. In common philosophical language, a proposition or _____, is the content of an assertion, that is, it is true-or-false and defined by the meaning of a particular piece of language.
   a. Statement0
   b. Concept
   c. Undefined
   d. Undefined

Chapter 6. INTEGRATION

77. _____ variables are variables other than the independent variable that may bear any effect on the behavior of the subject being studied.
   a. Thing
   b. Extraneous0
   c. Undefined
   d. Undefined

78. In mathematics, the _____ of two sets A and B is the set that contains all elements of A that also belong to B (or equivalently, all elements of B that also belong to A), but no other elements.
   a. Thing
   b. Intersection0
   c. Undefined
   d. Undefined

79. Initial objects are also called _____, and terminal objects are also called final.
   a. Coterminal0
   b. Thing
   c. Undefined
   d. Undefined

80. In mathematics, in the field of differential equations, an initial value problem is a differential equation together with specified value, called the _____, of the unknown function at a given point in the domain of the solution.
   a. Initial condition0
   b. Thing
   c. Undefined
   d. Undefined

81. _____ of an object is its speed in a particular direction.
   a. Thing
   b. Velocity0
   c. Undefined
   d. Undefined

82. _____ or arithmetics is the oldest and most elementary branch of mathematics, used by almost everyone, for tasks ranging from simple daily counting to advanced science and business calculations.
   a. Thing
   b. Arithmetic0
   c. Undefined
   d. Undefined

83. In mathematics, the _____ of a coordinate system is the point where the axes of the system intersect.
   a. Origin0
   b. Thing
   c. Undefined
   d. Undefined

84. The _____ (symbol _____) and the millibar (symbol mbar, also mb) are units of pressure.
   a. Bar0
   b. Thing
   c. Undefined
   d. Undefined

85. _____ is the force that opposes the relative motion or tendency toward such motion of two surfaces in contact.
   a. Friction0
   b. Thing
   c. Undefined
   d. Undefined

86. _____ algebra (sometimes called General algebra) is the field of mathematics that studies the ideas common to all algebraic structures.
   a. Universal0
   b. Thing
   c. Undefined
   d. Undefined

Chapter 6. INTEGRATION

87. In mathematics, _____ geometry was the traditional name for the geometry of three-dimensional Euclidean space — for practical purposes the kind of space we live in.
    a. Thing
    b. Solid0
    c. Undefined
    d. Undefined

88. In mathematics, a _____ is a quadric surface, with the following equation in Cartesian coordinates: $(x/_a)^2 + (y/_b)^2 = 1$.
    a. Cylinder0
    b. Thing
    c. Undefined
    d. Undefined

89. The term _____ refers to the largest and the smallest element of a set.
    a. Extreme value0
    b. Thing
    c. Undefined
    d. Undefined

90. _____ is a means of calculating the volume of a solid of revolution, when integrating along the axis of revolution. This method models the generated 3 dimensional shape as a "stack" of an infinite number of disks of infinitesimal thickness.
    a. Disk method0
    b. Thing
    c. Undefined
    d. Undefined

91. In geometry, a _____ is the intersection of a body in 2-dimensional space with a line, or of a body in 3-dimensional space with a plane
    a. Thing
    b. Cross section0
    c. Undefined
    d. Undefined

92. In mathematics, a _____ is a two-dimensional manifold or surface that is perfectly flat.
    a. Thing
    b. Plane0
    c. Undefined
    d. Undefined

93. In mathematics, a _____ is the set of all points in three-dimensional space (R^3) which are at distance r from a fixed point of that space, where r is a positive real number called the radius of the _____. The fixed point is called the center or centre, and is not part of the _____ itself.
    a. Sphere0
    b. Thing
    c. Undefined
    d. Undefined

94. In geometry, two lines or planes if one falls on the other in such a way as to create congruent adjacent angles. The term may be used as a noun or adjective. Thus, referring to Figure 1, the line AB is the _____ to CD through the point B.
    a. Perpendicular0
    b. Thing
    c. Undefined
    d. Undefined

95. A _____ is a movement of an object in a circular motion. A two-dimensional object rotates around a center (or point) of _____. A three-dimensional object rotates around a line called an axis. If the axis of _____ is within the body, the body is said to rotate upon itself, or spin—which implies relative speed and perhaps free-movement with angular momentum. A circular motion about an external point, e.g. the Earth about the Sun, is called an orbit or more properly an orbital revolution.

a. Thing b. Rotation0
c. Undefined d. Undefined

96. _____, verti-bar, vertical line, divider line, or pipe is the name of the character .
 a. Vertical bar0 b. Thing
 c. Undefined d. Undefined

97. _____ is a relation in Euclidean geometry among the three sides of a right triangle.
 a. Thing b. Pythagorean Theorem0
 c. Undefined d. Undefined

98. In geometry a _____ is a plane figure that is bounded by a closed path or circuit, composed of a finite number of sequential line segments.
 a. Thing b. Polygon0
 c. Undefined d. Undefined

99. In geometry, a line _____ is a part of a line that is bounded by two end points, and contains every point on the line between its end points.
 a. Segment0 b. Concept
 c. Undefined d. Undefined

100. A _____ is a part of a line that is bounded by two end points, and contains every point on the line between its end points.
 a. Line segment0 b. Thing
 c. Undefined d. Undefined

101. In plane geometry, a _____ is a polygon with four equal sides, four right angles, and parallel opposite sides. In algebra, the _____ of a number is that number multiplied by itself.
 a. Square0 b. Thing
 c. Undefined d. Undefined

102. The term _____ can refer to an integer which is the square of some other integer, or an algebraic expression that can be factored as the square of some other expression.
 a. Thing b. Perfect square0
 c. Undefined d. Undefined

103. In mathematics, a _____ is a type of conic section defined as the intersection between a right circular conical surface and a plane which cuts through both halves of the cone.
 a. Hyperbola0 b. Thing
 c. Undefined d. Undefined

104. _____ is a differential equation together with specified value, called the initial condition, of the unknown function at a given point in the domain of the solution.
 a. Initial value problem0 b. Thing
 c. Undefined d. Undefined

Chapter 6. INTEGRATION

105. In sociology and biology a _____ is the collection of people or organisms of a particular species living in a given geographic area or space, usually measured by a census.
   a. Population0
   b. Thing
   c. Undefined
   d. Undefined

106. _____ is a physical property of a system that underlies the common notions of hot and cold; something that is hotter has the greater _____.
   a. Temperature0
   b. Thing
   c. Undefined
   d. Undefined

107. _____ is a synonym for information.
   a. Thing
   b. Data0
   c. Undefined
   d. Undefined

108. _____ is defined as the rate of change or derivative with respect to time of velocity.
   a. Thing
   b. Acceleration0
   c. Undefined
   d. Undefined

109. A _____ is a three-dimensional geometric shape formed by straight lines through a fixed point (vertex) to the points of a fixed curve (directrix)
   a. Cone0
   b. Concept
   c. Undefined
   d. Undefined

110. An n-sided _____ is a polyhedron formed by connecting an n-sided polygonal base and a point, called the apex, by n triangular faces. In other words, it is a conic solid with polygonal base.
   a. Thing
   b. Pyramid0
   c. Undefined
   d. Undefined

111. _____ is the shape of a hanging flexible chain or cable when supported at its ends and acted upon by a uniform gravitational force. The chain is steepest near the points of suspension because this part of the chain has the most weight pulling down on it. Toward the bottom, the slope of the chain decreases because the chain is supporting less weight.
   a. Thing
   b. Catenary0
   c. Undefined
   d. Undefined

112. In Euclidean geometry, an _____ is a closed segment of a differentiable curve in the two-dimensional plane; for example, a circular _____ is a segment of a circle.
   a. Concept
   b. Arc0
   c. Undefined
   d. Undefined

113. A _____ of a number is the product of that number with any integer.
   a. Multiple0
   b. Thing
   c. Undefined
   d. Undefined

114. In set theory and other branches of mathematics, the _____ of a collection of sets is the set that contains everything that belongs to any of the sets, but nothing else.

Chapter 6. INTEGRATION

a. Union0
b. Thing
c. Undefined
d. Undefined

115. In calculus, the _____ in differentiation is a method of finding the derivative of a function that is the sum of two other functions for which derivatives exist.
a. Thing
b. Sum Rule0
c. Undefined
d. Undefined

116. _____ is the addition of a set of numbers; the result is their sum. The "numbers" to be summed may be natural numbers, complex numbers, matrices, or still more complicated objects. An infinite sum is a subtle procedure known as a series.
a. Summation0
b. Thing
c. Undefined
d. Undefined

117. _____ also called rectification of a curve—was historically difficult.
a. Arc length0
b. Thing
c. Undefined
d. Undefined

118. _____ is a kind of property which exists as magnitude or multitude. It is among the basic classes of things along with quality, substance, change, and relation.
a. Amount0
b. Thing
c. Undefined
d. Undefined

119. A _____ is traditionally an infinitesimally small change in a variable.
a. Differential0
b. Thing
c. Undefined
d. Undefined

120. _____ is the estimation of a physical quantity such as distance, energy, temperature, or time.
a. Thing
b. Measurement0
c. Undefined
d. Undefined

Chapter 7. INTEGRATION TECHNIQUES AND COMPUTATIONAL METHODS

1. In mathematics, a _____ is the result of multiplying, or an expression that identifies factors to be multiplied.
   a. Thing
   b. Product0
   c. Undefined
   d. Undefined

2. The _____ governs the differentiation of products of differentiable functions.
   a. Thing
   b. Product rule0
   c. Undefined
   d. Undefined

3. _____ is a process of combining or accumulating. It may also refer to:
   a. Integration0
   b. Thing
   c. Undefined
   d. Undefined

4. In calculus, the _____ is a formula for the derivative of the composite of two functions.
   a. Concept
   b. Chain rule0
   c. Undefined
   d. Undefined

5. The _____ is a tool for finding antiderivatives and integrals. It is the counterpart to the chain rule of differentiation.
   a. Thing
   b. Substitution rule0
   c. Undefined
   d. Undefined

6. The _____ of a function is an extension of the concept of a sum, and are identified or found through the use of integration.
   a. Integral0
   b. Thing
   c. Undefined
   d. Undefined

7. A _____ is a symbolic representation denoting a quantity or expression. It often represents an "unknown" quantity that has the potential to change.
   a. Thing
   b. Variable0
   c. Undefined
   d. Undefined

8. Mathematical _____ is used to represent ideas.
   a. Thing
   b. Notation0
   c. Undefined
   d. Undefined

9. _____ was a German mathematician and philosopher. He invented calculus independently of Newton, and his notation is the one in general use since.
   a. Leibniz0
   b. Person
   c. Undefined
   d. Undefined

10. _____ named in honor of the 17th century German philosopher and mathematician Gottfried Wilhelm Leibniz, was originally the use of expressions such as dx and dy and to represent "infinitely small" or infinitesimal increments of quantities x and y, just as Äx and Äy represent finite increments of x and y respectively.
    a. Thing
    b. Leibniz notation0
    c. Undefined
    d. Undefined

Chapter 7. INTEGRATION TECHNIQUES AND COMPUTATIONAL METHODS

11. The mathematical concept of a _____ expresses the intuitive idea of deterministic dependence between two quantities, one of which is viewed as primary and the other as secondary. A _____ then is a way to associate a unique output for each input of a specified type, for example, a real number or an element of a given set.
    a. Thing
    b. Function0
    c. Undefined
    d. Undefined

12. A _____ signifies a point or points of probability on a subject e.g., the _____ of creativity, which allows for the formation of rule or norm or law by interpretation of the phenomena events that can be created.
    a. Thing
    b. Principle0
    c. Undefined
    d. Undefined

13. The _____ is a measurement of how a function changes when the values of its inputs change.
    a. Derivative0
    b. Thing
    c. Undefined
    d. Undefined

14. In mathematics, the _____ inverse of a number x, denoted 1/x or x^{-1}, is the number which, when multiplied by x, yields 1. The _____ inverse of x is also called the reciprocal of x.
    a. Multiplicative0
    b. Thing
    c. Undefined
    d. Undefined

15. _____ is a function that extends the concept of an ordinary sum
    a. Thing
    b. Integrand0
    c. Undefined
    d. Undefined

16. In mathematics and the mathematical sciences, a _____ is a fixed, but possibly unspecified, value. This is in contrast to a variable, which is not fixed.
    a. Thing
    b. Constant0
    c. Undefined
    d. Undefined

17. In plane geometry, a _____ is a polygon with four equal sides, four right angles, and parallel opposite sides. In algebra, the _____ of a number is that number multiplied by itself.
    a. Thing
    b. Square0
    c. Undefined
    d. Undefined

18. In mathematics, a _____ of a number x is a number r such that r^2 = x, or in words, a number r whose square (the result of multiplying the number by itself) is x.
    a. Square root0
    b. Thing
    c. Undefined
    d. Undefined

19. In mathematics, a _____ of a complex-valued function f is a member x of the domain of f such that f(x) vanishes at x, that is, x : f (x) = 0.
    a. Root0
    b. Thing
    c. Undefined
    d. Undefined

20. A _____ function is a function for which, intuitively, small changes in the input result in small changes in the output.

Chapter 7. INTEGRATION TECHNIQUES AND COMPUTATIONAL METHODS

a. Continuous0
b. Event
c. Undefined
d. Undefined

21. _____ is an extension of the concept of a sum.
    a. Definite integral0
    b. Thing
    c. Undefined
    d. Undefined

22. An _____ of a function f is a function F whose derivative is equal to f, i.e., F' = f.
    a. Antiderivative0
    b. Thing
    c. Undefined
    d. Undefined

23. In mathematics, an inequality is a statement about the relative size or order of two objects. For example 14 > 10, or 14 is _____ 10.
    a. Thing
    b. Greater than0
    c. Undefined
    d. Undefined

24. A _____ is a function for which, intuitively, small changes in the input result in small changes in the output.
    a. Continuous function0
    b. Event
    c. Undefined
    d. Undefined

25. _____ is a trigonemtric function that is important when studying triangles and modeling periodic phenomena, among other applications.
    a. Sine0
    b. Thing
    c. Undefined
    d. Undefined

26. The _____, the average in everyday English, which is also called the arithmetic _____ (and is distinguished from the geometric _____ or harmonic _____). The average is also called the sample _____. The expected value of a random variable, which is also called the population _____.
    a. Thing
    b. Mean0
    c. Undefined
    d. Undefined

27. _____ has many meanings, most of which simply .
    a. Thing
    b. Power0
    c. Undefined
    d. Undefined

28. In calculus, the indefinite integral of a given function i.e. the set of all antiderivatives of the function is always written with a constant, the _____.
    a. Thing
    b. Constant of integration0
    c. Undefined
    d. Undefined

29. In common philosophical language, a proposition or _____, is the content of an assertion, that is, it is true-or-false and defined by the meaning of a particular piece of language.
    a. Concept
    b. Statement0
    c. Undefined
    d. Undefined

Chapter 7. INTEGRATION TECHNIQUES AND COMPUTATIONAL METHODS

30. In algebra, the _____ decomposition or _____ expansion is used to reduce the degree of either the numerator or the denominator of a rational function.
    a. Partial fraction0
    b. Thing
    c. Undefined
    d. Undefined

31. In mathematics, _____ refers to the rewriting of an expression into a simpler form.
    a. Reduction0
    b. Thing
    c. Undefined
    d. Undefined

32. An _____ is a combination of numbers, operators, grouping symbols and/or free variables and bound variables arranged in a meaningful way which can be evaluated..
    a. Thing
    b. Expression0
    c. Undefined
    d. Undefined

33. A _____ is the part of a fraction that tells how many equal parts make up a whole, and which is used in the name of the fraction: "halves", "thirds", "fourths" or "quarters", "fifths" and so on.
    a. Denominator0
    b. Concept
    c. Undefined
    d. Undefined

34. In mathematics, a _____ is the end result of a division problem. It can also be expressed as the number of times the divisor divides into the dividend.
    a. Thing
    b. Quotient0
    c. Undefined
    d. Undefined

35. In mathematics, a _____ number is a number which can be expressed as a ratio of two integers. Non-integer _____ numbers (commonly called fractions) are usually written as the vulgar fraction a / b, where b is not zero.
    a. Rational0
    b. Thing
    c. Undefined
    d. Undefined

36. In mathematics, a _____ is any function which can be written as the ratio of two polynomial functions.
    a. Rational function0
    b. Thing
    c. Undefined
    d. Undefined

37. In mathematics, a _____ is an expression that is constructed from one or more variables and constants, using only the operations of addition, subtraction, multiplication, and constant positive whole number exponents. is a _____. Note in particular that division by an expression containing a variable is not in general allowed in polynomials. [1]
    a. Thing
    b. Polynomial0
    c. Undefined
    d. Undefined

38. A _____ is the result of the addition of a set of numbers. The numbers may be natural numbers, complex numbers, matrices, or still more complicated objects. An infinite _____ is a subtle procedure known as a series.
    a. Thing
    b. Sum0
    c. Undefined
    d. Undefined

39. A _____ fraction is a fraction in which the absolute value of the numerator is less than the denominator--hence, the absolute value of the fraction is less than 1.

Chapter 7. INTEGRATION TECHNIQUES AND COMPUTATIONAL METHODS

    a. Thing
    c. Undefined
    b. Proper0
    d. Undefined

40. A _____ is a numeral used to indicate a count. The most common use of the word today is to name the part of a fraction that tells the number or count of equal parts.
    a. Numerator0
    c. Undefined
    b. Thing
    d. Undefined

41. In arithmetic, _____ is a procedure for calculating the division of one integer, called the dividend, by another integer called the divisor, to produce a result called the quotient.
    a. Long division0
    c. Undefined
    b. Thing
    d. Undefined

42. In mathematics, there are several meanings of _____ depending on the subject.
    a. Degree0
    c. Undefined
    b. Thing
    d. Undefined

43. A quadratic equation with real solutions, called roots, which may be real or complex, is given by the _____ : $x = \frac{-b \pm \sqrt{b^2 - 4ac}}{2a}$.
    a. Thing
    c. Undefined
    b. Quadratic formula0
    d. Undefined

44. In mathematics, factorization (British English: factorisation) or factoring is the decomposition of an object (for example, a number, a polynomial, or a matrix) into a product of other objects, or _____, which when multiplied together give the original.
    a. Thing
    c. Undefined
    b. Factors0
    d. Undefined

45. The word _____ comes from the Latin word linearis, which means created by lines.
    a. Linear0
    c. Undefined
    b. Thing
    d. Undefined

46. _____ is a branch of mathematics concerning the study of structure, relation and quantity.
    a. Concept
    c. Undefined
    b. Algebra0
    d. Undefined

47. _____ refers to the reduction of the body of a formerly living organism into simpler forms of matter.
    a. Decomposing0
    c. Undefined
    b. Thing
    d. Undefined

48. In mathematics, _____ is the decomposition of an object into a product of other objects, or factors, which when multiplied together give the original.
    a. Thing
    c. Undefined
    b. Factoring0
    d. Undefined

Chapter 7. INTEGRATION TECHNIQUES AND COMPUTATIONAL METHODS

49. A _____ is a first degree polynomial mathematical function of the form: f(x) = mx + b where m and b are real constants and x is a real variable.
- a. Linear function0
- b. Thing
- c. Undefined
- d. Undefined

50. In mathematics, _____ expressions is used to reduce the expression into the lowest possible term.
- a. Thing
- b. Simplifying0
- c. Undefined
- d. Undefined

51. An _____ is the limit of a definite integral, as an endpoint of the interval of integration approaches either a specified real number or ‡ or − ‡ or, in some cases, as both endpoints approach limits.
- a. Thing
- b. Improper integral0
- c. Undefined
- d. Undefined

52. In mathematics, a set is called _____ if there is a bijection between the set and some set of the form {1, 2, ..., n} where n is a natural number.
- a. Finite0
- b. Thing
- c. Undefined
- d. Undefined

53. _____ is the state of being greater than any finite number, however large.
- a. Infinity0
- b. Thing
- c. Undefined
- d. Undefined

54. In elementary algebra, an _____ is a set that contains every real number between two indicated numbers and may contain the two numbers themselves.
- a. Interval0
- b. Thing
- c. Undefined
- d. Undefined

55. In mathematics, a _____ may be described informally as a number that can be given by an infinite decimal representation.
- a. Real number0
- b. Thing
- c. Undefined
- d. Undefined

56. In mathematics, _____ describes an entity with a limit.
- a. Convergent0
- b. Thing
- c. Undefined
- d. Undefined

57. _____ Any process by which a specified characteristic usually amplitude of the output of a device is prevented from exceeding a predetermined value.
- a. Limiting0
- b. Thing
- c. Undefined
- d. Undefined

58. _____ is the state of being greater than any finite real or natural number, however large.
- a. Thing
- b. Infinite0
- c. Undefined
- d. Undefined

Chapter 7. INTEGRATION TECHNIQUES AND COMPUTATIONAL METHODS

59. In mathematics, defined and _____ are used to explain whether or not expressions have meaningful, sensible, and unambiguous values.
    a. Undefined0
    b. Thing
    c. Undefined
    d. Undefined

60. In geometry, an _____ is a point at which a line segment or ray terminates.
    a. Endpoint0
    b. Thing
    c. Undefined
    d. Undefined

61. In mathematics, a _____ series is an infinite series that is not convergent, meaning that the infinite sequence of the partial sums of the series does not have a limit.
    a. Divergent0
    b. Thing
    c. Undefined
    d. Undefined

62. _____ denotes the approach toward a definite value, as time goes on; or to a definite point, a common view or opinion, or toward a fixed or equilibrium state.
    a. Thing
    b. Convergence0
    c. Undefined
    d. Undefined

63. _____ constitutes a broad family of algorithms for calculating the numerical value of a definite integral, and by extension, the term is also sometimes used to describe the numerical solution of differential equations.
    a. Thing
    b. Numerical integration0
    c. Undefined
    d. Undefined

64. Initial objects are also called _____, and terminal objects are also called final.
    a. Thing
    b. Coterminal0
    c. Undefined
    d. Undefined

65. In geometry, a _____ is defined as a quadrilateral where all four of its angles are right angles.
    a. Rectangle0
    b. Thing
    c. Undefined
    d. Undefined

66. _____ is a method for approximating the values of integrals.
    a. Riemann sum0
    b. Thing
    c. Undefined
    d. Undefined

67. In mathematics, a _____ is an ordered list of objects. Like a set, it contains members, also called elements or terms, and the number of terms is called the length of the _____. Unlike a set, order matters, and the exact same elements can appear multiple times at different positions in the _____.
    a. Thing
    b. Sequence0
    c. Undefined
    d. Undefined

68. Generally, a _____ is a splitting of something into parts.
    a. Thing
    b. Partition0
    c. Undefined
    d. Undefined

Chapter 7. INTEGRATION TECHNIQUES AND COMPUTATIONAL METHODS

69. _____ is the middle point of a line segment.
    a. Thing
    b. Midpoint0
    c. Undefined
    d. Undefined

70. In mathematics, especially in order theory, an _____ of a subset S of some partially ordered set is an element of P which is greater than or equal to every element of S.
    a. Upper bound0
    b. Thing
    c. Undefined
    d. Undefined

71. In mathematics, the word _____ is used informally to refer to certain distinct bodies of knowledge about mathematics.
    a. Thing
    b. Theoretical0
    c. Undefined
    d. Undefined

72. _____ is the fee paid on borrowed money.
    a. Thing
    b. Interest0
    c. Undefined
    d. Undefined

73. A _____ is a quadrilateral, which is defined as a shape with four sides, which has a pair of parallel sides.
    a. Trapezoid0
    b. Thing
    c. Undefined
    d. Undefined

74. _____ the American term is a way to approximately calculate the definite integral
    a. Thing
    b. Trapezoidal Rule0
    c. Undefined
    d. Undefined

75. The term _____ is defined dually as an element of P which is lesser than or equal to every element of S.
    a. Thing
    b. Lower bound0
    c. Undefined
    d. Undefined

76. The _____ integers are all the integers from zero on upwards.
    a. Thing
    b. Nonnegative0
    c. Undefined
    d. Undefined

77. A _____ is a set of numbers that designate location in a given reference system, such as x,y in a planar _____ system or an x,y,z in a three-dimensional _____ system.
    a. Coordinate0
    b. Thing
    c. Undefined
    d. Undefined

78. In mathematics and its applications, a _____ is a system for assigning an n-tuple of numbers or scalars to each point in an n-dimensional space.
    a. Concept
    b. Coordinate system0
    c. Undefined
    d. Undefined

79. _____ is an approximation of a general function using a linear function more precisely, an affine function.

Chapter 7. INTEGRATION TECHNIQUES AND COMPUTATIONAL METHODS

    a. Thing
    c. Undefined
    b. Linear approximation0
    d. Undefined

80. In mathematics and its applications, _____ refers to finding the linear approximation to a function at a given point.
    a. Linearization0
    c. Undefined
    b. Thing
    d. Undefined

81. In mathematics, a _____ is a constant multiplicative factor of a certain object. The object can be such things as a variable, a vector, a function, etc. For example, the _____ of $9x^2$ is 9.
    a. Coefficient0
    c. Undefined
    b. Thing
    d. Undefined

82. _____ are the basic objects of study in graph theory. Informally speaking, a graph is a set of objects called points, nodes, or vertices connected by links called lines or edges.
    a. Graphs0
    c. Undefined
    b. Thing
    d. Undefined

83. In mathematics, the _____ is a representation of a function as an infinite sum of terms calculated from the values of its derivatives at a single point.
    a. Taylor series0
    c. Undefined
    b. Thing
    d. Undefined

84. In sociology and biology a _____ is the collection of people or organisms of a particular species living in a given geographic area or space, usually measured by a census.
    a. Population0
    c. Undefined
    b. Thing
    d. Undefined

85. In mathematics, _____ growth occurs when the growth rate of a function is always proportional to the function's current size.
    a. Exponential0
    c. Undefined
    b. Thing
    d. Undefined

86. A _____ is a special kind of ratio, indicating a relationship between two measurements with different units, such as miles to gallons or cents to pounds.
    a. Thing
    c. Undefined
    b. Rate0
    d. Undefined

87. One of the three formats applicable to a quadratic function is the _____ which is defined as $f = ax^2 + bx + c$.
    a. General form0
    c. Undefined
    b. Thing
    d. Undefined

88. The deductive-nomological model is a formalized view of scientific _____ in natural language.
    a. Thing
    c. Undefined
    b. Explanation0
    d. Undefined

Chapter 7. INTEGRATION TECHNIQUES AND COMPUTATIONAL METHODS

89. _____ is an operator that measures the magnitude of a vector field's source or sink at a given point; the _____ of a vector field is a signed scalar.
   a. Divergence0
   b. Thing
   c. Undefined
   d. Undefined

90. In statistics the _____ of an event i is the number n_i of times the event occurred in the experiment or the study. These frequencies are often graphically represented in histograms.
   a. Frequency0
   b. Concept
   c. Undefined
   d. Undefined

91. In mathematics, an _____, mean, or central tendency of a data set refers to a measure of the "middle" or "expected" value of the data set.
   a. Concept
   b. Average0
   c. Undefined
   d. Undefined

Chapter 8. DIFFERENTIAL EQUATIONS

1. In mathematics, two quantities are called _____ if they vary in such a way that one of the quantities is a constant multiple of the other, or equivalently if they have a constant ratio.
   - a. Thing
   - b. Proportional0
   - c. Undefined
   - d. Undefined

2. A _____ is a special kind of ratio, indicating a relationship between two measurements with different units, such as miles to gallons or cents to pounds.
   - a. Thing
   - b. Rate0
   - c. Undefined
   - d. Undefined

3. In sociology and biology a _____ is the collection of people or organisms of a particular species living in a given geographic area or space, usually measured by a census.
   - a. Thing
   - b. Population0
   - c. Undefined
   - d. Undefined

4. _____ is change in population over time, and can be quantified as the change in the number of individuals in a population per unit time.
   - a. Thing
   - b. Population growth0
   - c. Undefined
   - d. Undefined

5. A _____ is traditionally an infinitesimally small change in a variable.
   - a. Thing
   - b. Differential0
   - c. Undefined
   - d. Undefined

6. The _____ is a measurement of how a function changes when the values of its inputs change.
   - a. Derivative0
   - b. Thing
   - c. Undefined
   - d. Undefined

7. A _____ is a mathematical equation for an unknown function of one or several variables which relates the values of the function itself and of its derivatives of various orders.
   - a. Thing
   - b. Differential equation0
   - c. Undefined
   - d. Undefined

8. The mathematical concept of a _____ expresses the intuitive idea of deterministic dependence between two quantities, one of which is viewed as primary and the other as secondary. A _____ then is a way to associate a unique output for each input of a specified type, for example, a real number or an element of a given set.
   - a. Function0
   - b. Thing
   - c. Undefined
   - d. Undefined

9. A _____ is a symbolic representation denoting a quantity or expression. It often represents an "unknown" quantity that has the potential to change.
   - a. Thing
   - b. Variable0
   - c. Undefined
   - d. Undefined

10. In mathematics, a _____ function in the sense of algebraic geometry is an everywhere-defined, polynomial function on an algebraic variety V with values in the field K over which V is defined.

Chapter 8. DIFFERENTIAL EQUATIONS

   a. Thing
   c. Undefined
   b. Regular0
   d. Undefined

11. In mathematics, the concept of a _____ tries to capture the intuitive idea of a geometrical one-dimensional and continuous object. A simple example is the circle.
   a. Curve0
   c. Undefined
   b. Thing
   d. Undefined

12. _____ is the path a moving object follows through space.
   a. Projectile motion0
   c. Undefined
   b. Thing
   d. Undefined

13. The _____ of measurement are a globally standardized and modernized form of the metric system.
   a. Units0
   c. Undefined
   b. Thing
   d. Undefined

14. Initial objects are also called _____, and terminal objects are also called final.
   a. Thing
   c. Undefined
   b. Coterminal0
   d. Undefined

15. In the scientific method, an _____ (Latin: ex-+-periri, "of (or from) trying"), is a set of actions and observations, performed in the context of solving a particular problem or question, in order to support or falsify a hypothesis or research concerning phenomena.
   a. Experiment0
   c. Undefined
   b. Thing
   d. Undefined

16. The _____, the average in everyday English, which is also called the arithmetic _____ (and is distinguished from the geometric _____ or harmonic _____). The average is also called the sample _____. The expected value of a random variable, which is also called the population _____.
   a. Thing
   c. Undefined
   b. Mean0
   d. Undefined

17. In mathematics and the mathematical sciences, a _____ is a fixed, but possibly unspecified, value. This is in contrast to a variable, which is not fixed.
   a. Constant0
   c. Undefined
   b. Thing
   d. Undefined

18. _____ is a process of combining or accumulating. It may also refer to:
   a. Thing
   c. Undefined
   b. Integration0
   d. Undefined

19. _____ is a function whose values do not vary and thus are constant.
   a. Thing
   c. Undefined
   b. Constant function0
   d. Undefined

20. In mathematics, _____ are the intuitive idea of a geometrical one-dimensional and continuous object.

Chapter 8. DIFFERENTIAL EQUATIONS

a. Curves0
b. Thing
c. Undefined
d. Undefined

21. _____ is the process in which an unstable atomic nucleus loses energy by emitting radiation in the form of particles or electromagnetic waves.
   a. Radioactive decay0
   b. Thing
   c. Undefined
   d. Undefined

22. _____ is a special mathematical relationship between two quantities. Two quantities are called proportional if they vary in such a way that one of the quantities is a constant multiple of the other, or equivalently if they have a constant ratio.
   a. Thing
   b. Proportionality0
   c. Undefined
   d. Undefined

23. _____ is a method of describing limiting behavior.
   a. Asymptotic0
   b. Thing
   c. Undefined
   d. Undefined

24. A _____ is the quantity that defines certain relatively constant characteristics of systems or functions..
   a. Thing
   b. Parameter0
   c. Undefined
   d. Undefined

25. A _____ is 360° or 2𝛿 radians.
   a. Turn0
   b. Thing
   c. Undefined
   d. Undefined

26. In mathematics, in the field of differential equations, an initial value problem is a differential equation together with specified value, called the _____, of the unknown function at a given point in the domain of the solution.
   a. Initial condition0
   b. Thing
   c. Undefined
   d. Undefined

27. An _____ of a function f is a function F whose derivative is equal to f, i.e., F' = f.
   a. Thing
   b. Antiderivative0
   c. Undefined
   d. Undefined

28. In algebra, the _____ decomposition or _____ expansion is used to reduce the degree of either the numerator or the denominator of a rational function.
   a. Thing
   b. Partial fraction0
   c. Undefined
   d. Undefined

29. _____ is mass m per unit volume V.
   a. Thing
   b. Density0
   c. Undefined
   d. Undefined

30. In geographic information systems, a _____ comprises an entity with a geographic location, typically determined by points, arcs, or polygons. Carriageways and cadastres exemplify _____ data.

Chapter 8. DIFFERENTIAL EQUATIONS

a. Feature0
b. Thing
c. Undefined
d. Undefined

31. Pierre François _____ was a mathematician and a doctor in number theory from the University of Ghent in 1825.
    a. Person
    b. Verhulst0
    c. Undefined
    d. Undefined

32. A _____ is the sum of the elements of a sequence.
    a. Series0
    b. Thing
    c. Undefined
    d. Undefined

33. _____ was an American biologist, who spent most of his career at Johns Hopkins University in Baltimore.
    a. Raymond Pearl0
    b. Person
    c. Undefined
    d. Undefined

34. In economics _____ means before deductions brutto, e.g. _____ domestic or national product, or _____ profit or income
    a. Thing
    b. Gross0
    c. Undefined
    d. Undefined

35. _____ is a synonym for information.
    a. Data0
    b. Thing
    c. Undefined
    d. Undefined

36. _____ Any process by which a specified characteristic usually amplitude of the output of a device is prevented from exceeding a predetermined value.
    a. Thing
    b. Limiting0
    c. Undefined
    d. Undefined

37. _____ is a differential equation together with specified value, called the initial condition, of the unknown function at a given point in the domain of the solution.
    a. Thing
    b. Initial value problem0
    c. Undefined
    d. Undefined

38. _____ is the ability to hold, receive or absorb, or a measure thereof, similar to the concept of volume.
    a. Concept
    b. Capacity0
    c. Undefined
    d. Undefined

39. _____ usually refers to the biological _____ of a population level that can be supported for an organism, given the quantity of food, habitat, water and other life infrastructure present.
    a. Thing
    b. Carrying capacity0
    c. Undefined
    d. Undefined

40. In mathematics, an inequality is a statement about the relative size or order of two objects. For example 14 > 10, or 14 is _____ 10.

Chapter 8. DIFFERENTIAL EQUATIONS

a. Greater than0
c. Undefined
b. Thing
d. Undefined

41. The _____ of a solid object is the three-dimensional concept of how much space it occupies, often quantified numerically.
   a. Thing
   b. Volume0
   c. Undefined
   d. Undefined

42. A _____ is an individual or household that purchases and uses goods and services generated within the economy.
   a. Thing
   b. Consumer0
   c. Undefined
   d. Undefined

43. In mathematics, _____ expressions is used to reduce the expression into the lowest possible term.
   a. Simplifying0
   b. Thing
   c. Undefined
   d. Undefined

44. _____ is often used to describe the measurement of the steepness, incline, gradient, or grade of a straight line. The _____ is defined as the ratio of the "rise" divided by the "run" between two points on a line, or in other words, the ratio of the altitude change to the horizontal distance between any two points on the line.
   a. Thing
   b. Slope0
   c. Undefined
   d. Undefined

45. An _____ is a straight line around which a geometric figure can be rotated.
   a. Thing
   b. Axis0
   c. Undefined
   d. Undefined

46. In astronomy, geography, geometry and related sciences and contexts, a plane is said to be _____ at a given point if it is locally perpendicular to the gradient of the gravity field, i.e., with the direction of the gravitational force at that point.
   a. Horizontal0
   b. Thing
   c. Undefined
   d. Undefined

47. The word _____ comes from the Latin word linearis, which means created by lines.
   a. Linear0
   b. Thing
   c. Undefined
   d. Undefined

48. Any point where a graph makes contact with an coordinate axis is called an _____ of the graph
   a. Intercept0
   b. Thing
   c. Undefined
   d. Undefined

49. In Euclidean geometry, a uniform _____ is a linear transformation that enlargers or diminishes objects, and whose _____ factor is the same in all directions. This is also called homothethy.
   a. Thing
   b. Scale0
   c. Undefined
   d. Undefined

Chapter 8. DIFFERENTIAL EQUATIONS

50. _____ is a kind of property which exists as magnitude or multitude. It is among the basic classes of things along with quality, substance, change, and relation.
    a. Thing
    b. Amount0
    c. Undefined
    d. Undefined

51. _____ are a measure of time.
    a. Thing
    b. Minutes0
    c. Undefined
    d. Undefined

52. _____ was an Austrian-born biologist known as one of the founders of general systems theory.
    a. Von Bertalanffy0
    b. Person
    c. Undefined
    d. Undefined

53. An _____ is a combination of numbers, operators, grouping symbols and/or free variables and bound variables arranged in a meaningful way which can be evaluated..
    a. Expression0
    b. Thing
    c. Undefined
    d. Undefined

54. _____ is the property of a physical object that quantifies the amount of matter and energy it is equivalent to.
    a. Mass0
    b. Thing
    c. Undefined
    d. Undefined

55. In mathematics, an _____ is any of the arguments, i.e. "inputs", to a function. Thus if we have a function f(x), then x is a _____.
    a. Thing
    b. Independent variable0
    c. Undefined
    d. Undefined

56. In economics, economic _____ is simply a state of the world where economic forces are balanced and in the absence of external influences the values of economic variables will not change.
    a. Equilibrium0
    b. Thing
    c. Undefined
    d. Undefined

57. _____ is the fee paid on borrowed money.
    a. Interest0
    b. Thing
    c. Undefined
    d. Undefined

58. In physics, _____ is an influence that may cause an object to accelerate. It may be experienced as a lift, a push, or a pull. The actual acceleration of the body is determined by the vector sum of all forces acting on it, known as net _____ or resultant _____.
    a. Force0
    b. Thing
    c. Undefined
    d. Undefined

59. _____ is an approximation of a general function using a linear function more precisely, an affine function.
    a. Thing
    b. Linear approximation0
    c. Undefined
    d. Undefined

Chapter 8. DIFFERENTIAL EQUATIONS

60. A vector can be thought of as an arrow. It has a length, called its magnitude, and it points in some particular direction. A linear transformation inputs a vector and changes it, usually changing both its magnitude and its direction. An eigenvector of a given linear transformation is a vector which is simply multiplied by a constant called the _____ during that transformation.
   a. Thing
   b. Eigenvalue0
   c. Undefined
   d. Undefined

61. In trigonometry, the _____ is a function defined as $\tan x = \sin x / \cos x$. The function is so-named because it can be defined as the length of a certain segment of a _____ (in the geometric sense) to the unit circle. In plane geometry, a line is _____ to a curve, at some point, if both line and curve pass through the point with the same direction.
   a. Thing
   b. Tangent0
   c. Undefined
   d. Undefined

62. _____ has two distinct but etymologically-related meanings: one in geometry and one in trigonometry.
   a. Thing
   b. Tangent line0
   c. Undefined
   d. Undefined

63. In a mathematical proof or a syllogism, a _____ is a statement that is the logical consequence of preceding statements.
   a. Concept
   b. Conclusion0
   c. Undefined
   d. Undefined

64. _____, in economics and political economy, are the distributions or payments awarded to the various suppliers of the factors of production.
   a. Returns0
   b. Thing
   c. Undefined
   d. Undefined

65. _____ the expected value of a random variable displays the average or central value of the variable. It is a summary value of the distribution of the variable.
   a. Determining0
   b. Thing
   c. Undefined
   d. Undefined

66. In mathematics and its applications, _____ refers to finding the linear approximation to a function at a given point.
   a. Thing
   b. Linearization0
   c. Undefined
   d. Undefined

67. In mathematics, the word _____ is used informally to refer to certain distinct bodies of knowledge about mathematics.
   a. Theoretical0
   b. Thing
   c. Undefined
   d. Undefined

68. The plus and _____ signs are mathematical symbols used to represent the notions of positive and negative as well as the operations of addition and subtraction.
   a. Minus0
   b. Thing
   c. Undefined
   d. Undefined

Chapter 8. DIFFERENTIAL EQUATIONS

69. A _____ is a negotiable instrument instructing a financial institution to pay a specific amount of a specific currency from a specific demand account held in the maker/depositor's name with that institution. Both the maker and payee may be natural persons or legal entities.
   a. Thing
   b. Check0
   c. Undefined
   d. Undefined

70. _____ are the basic objects of study in graph theory. Informally speaking, a graph is a set of objects called points, nodes, or vertices connected by links called lines or edges.
   a. Thing
   b. Graphs0
   c. Undefined
   d. Undefined

71. In probability theory, _____ are various sets of outcomes (a subset of the sample space) to which a probability is assigned.
   a. Events0
   b. Thing
   c. Undefined
   d. Undefined

72. A _____ models the S-curve of growth of some set P. The initial stage of growth is approximately exponential; then, as saturation begins, the growth slows, and at maturity, growth stops.
   a. Thing
   b. Logistic function0
   c. Undefined
   d. Undefined

73. _____ is a a point on a curve at which the tangent crosses the curve itself.
   a. Inflection point0
   b. Thing
   c. Undefined
   d. Undefined

74. A _____ is a statement or claimt that a particular event will occur in the future in more certain terms than a forecast.
   a. Thing
   b. Prediction0
   c. Undefined
   d. Undefined

75. In set theory and its applications throughout mathematics, _____ are a collection of sets (or sometimes other mathematical objects) that can be unambiguously defined by a property that all its members share.
   a. Classes0
   b. Thing
   c. Undefined
   d. Undefined

76. _____ is the property of two events happening at the same time in at least one reference frame.
   a. Simultaneous0
   b. Thing
   c. Undefined
   d. Undefined

77. In mathematics, factorization (British English: factorisation) or factoring is the decomposition of an object (for example, a number, a polynomial, or a matrix) into a product of other objects, or _____, which when multiplied together give the original.
   a. Factors0
   b. Thing
   c. Undefined
   d. Undefined

78. In a function the _____, is the variable which is the value, i.e. the "output", of the function.

Chapter 8. DIFFERENTIAL EQUATIONS

    a. Thing
    c. Undefined
    b. Dependent variable0
    d. Undefined

79. The easiest _____ prime numbers resides in the use of the Sieve of Eratosthenes, an algorithm that discovers all prime numbers to a specified integer.
    a. Method for finding0
    c. Undefined
    b. Thing
    d. Undefined

80. In mathematics, a _____ is a two-dimensional manifold or surface that is perfectly flat.
    a. Plane0
    c. Undefined
    b. Thing
    d. Undefined

81. A _____ consists of one quarter of the coordinate plane.
    a. Thing
    c. Undefined
    b. Quadrant0
    d. Undefined

82. _____ is a straight line or curve A to which another curve B the one being studied approaches closer and closer as one moves along it.
    a. Thing
    c. Undefined
    b. Vertical asymptote0
    d. Undefined

83. An _____ is a straight line or curve A to which another curve B approaches closer and closer as one moves along it. As one moves along B, the space between it and the _____ A becomes smaller and smaller, and can in fact be made as small as one could wish by going far enough along. A curve may or may not touch or cross its _____. In fact, the curve may intersect the _____ an infinite number of times.
    a. Asymptote0
    c. Undefined
    b. Thing
    d. Undefined

84. In mathematics, an _____ is a statement about the relative size or order of two objects.
    a. Inequality0
    c. Undefined
    b. Thing
    d. Undefined

85. A _____ is the part of the dividend that is left over when the dividend is not evenly divisible by the divisor.
    a. Remainder0
    c. Undefined
    b. Thing
    d. Undefined

86. A _____ is the result of the addition of a set of numbers. The numbers may be natural numbers, complex numbers, matrices, or still more complicated objects. An infinite _____ is a subtle procedure known as a series.
    a. Thing
    c. Undefined
    b. Sum0
    d. Undefined

87. Sir Isaac _____, was an English physicist, mathematician, astronomer, natural philosopher, and alchemist, regarded by many as the greatest figure in the history of science
    a. Person
    c. Undefined
    b. Newton0
    d. Undefined

Chapter 8. DIFFERENTIAL EQUATIONS

88. _____ is a physical property of a system that underlies the common notions of hot and cold; something that is hotter has the greater _____.
 a. Temperature0
 b. Thing
 c. Undefined
 d. Undefined

89. In business, particularly accounting, a _____ is the time intervals that the accounts, statement, payments, or other calculations cover.
 a. Thing
 b. Period0
 c. Undefined
 d. Undefined

90. A central concept in science and the scientific method is that all evidence must be _____, or empirically based, that is, dependent on evidence or consequences that are observable by the senses.
 a. Thing
 b. Empirical0
 c. Undefined
 d. Undefined

91. The deductive-nomological model is a formalized view of scientific _____ in natural language.
 a. Thing
 b. Explanation0
 c. Undefined
 d. Undefined

92. In mathematics, _____ growth occurs when the growth rate of a function is always proportional to the function's current size.
 a. Exponential0
 b. Thing
 c. Undefined
 d. Undefined

93. _____ is electromagnetic radiation with a wavelength that is visible to the eye (visible _____) or, in a technical or scientific context, electromagnetic radiation of any wavelength.
 a. Light0
 b. Thing
 c. Undefined
 d. Undefined

Chapter 9. LINEAR ALCEBRA AND ANALYTIC GEOMETRY

1. The word _____ comes from the Latin word linearis, which means created by lines.
   a. Linear0
   b. Thing
   c. Undefined
   d. Undefined

2. _____ is a branch of mathematics concerning the study of structure, relation and quantity.
   a. Algebra0
   b. Concept
   c. Undefined
   d. Undefined

3. The _____ of measurement are a globally standardized and modernized form of the metric system.
   a. Units0
   b. Thing
   c. Undefined
   d. Undefined

4. In mathematics, an _____, mean, or central tendency of a data set refers to a measure of the "middle" or "expected" value of the data set.
   a. Average0
   b. Concept
   c. Undefined
   d. Undefined

5. A _____ is a symbolic representation denoting a quantity or expression. It often represents an "unknown" quantity that has the potential to change.
   a. Thing
   b. Variable0
   c. Undefined
   d. Undefined

6. A _____ is an equation in which each term is either a constant or the product of a constant times the first power of a variable.
   a. Linear equation0
   b. Thing
   c. Undefined
   d. Undefined

7. _____ is a notation for writing numbers that is often used by scientists and mathematicians to make it easier to write large and small numbers.
   a. Thing
   b. Scientific notation0
   c. Undefined
   d. Undefined

8. In mathematics and the mathematical sciences, a _____ is a fixed, but possibly unspecified, value. This is in contrast to a variable, which is not fixed.
   a. Constant0
   b. Thing
   c. Undefined
   d. Undefined

9. An _____ is a collection of two not necessarily distinct objects, one of which is distinguished as the first coordinate and the other as the second coordinate.
   a. Ordered pair0
   b. Thing
   c. Undefined
   d. Undefined

10. The _____, the average in everyday English, which is also called the arithmetic _____ (and is distinguished from the geometric _____ or harmonic _____). The average is also called the sample _____. The expected value of a random variable, which is also called the population _____.

a. Mean0
b. Thing
c. Undefined
d. Undefined

11. In mathematics, the _____ of two sets A and B is the set that contains all elements of A that also belong to B (or equivalently, all elements of B that also belong to A), but no other elements.
   a. Thing
   b. Intersection0
   c. Undefined
   d. Undefined

12. _____ is often used to describe the measurement of the steepness, incline, gradient, or grade of a straight line. The _____ is defined as the ratio of the "rise" divided by the "run" between two points on a line, or in other words, the ratio of the altitude change to the horizontal distance between any two points on the line.
   a. Thing
   b. Slope0
   c. Undefined
   d. Undefined

13. The existence and properties of _____ are the basis of Euclid's parallel postulate. _____ are two lines on the same plane that do not intersect even assuming that lines extend to infinity in either direction.
   a. Thing
   b. Parallel lines0
   c. Undefined
   d. Undefined

14. Equivalence is the condition of being _____ or essentially equal.
   a. Thing
   b. Equivalent0
   c. Undefined
   d. Undefined

15. A _____ is one of the basic shapes of geometry: a polygon with three vertices and three sides which are straight line segments.
   a. Triangle0
   b. Thing
   c. Undefined
   d. Undefined

16. A _____ is a number, figure, or indicator that appears below the normal line of type, typically used in a formula, mathematical expression, or description of a chemical compound.
   a. Thing
   b. Subscript0
   c. Undefined
   d. Undefined

17. In mathematics, a _____ is a constant multiplicative factor of a certain object. The object can be such things as a variable, a vector, a function, etc. For example, the _____ of $9x^2$ is 9.
   a. Coefficient0
   b. Thing
   c. Undefined
   d. Undefined

18. _____ is a special kind of square matrix where the entries below or above the main diagonal are zero.
   a. Triangular form0
   b. Thing
   c. Undefined
   d. Undefined

19. A _____ is a deliberate process for transforming one or more inputs into one or more results.
   a. Thing
   b. Calculation0
   c. Undefined
   d. Undefined

Chapter 9. LINEAR ALGEBRA AND ANALYTIC GEOMETRY

20. Mathematical _____ is used to represent ideas.
    a. Thing
    b. Notation0
    c. Undefined
    d. Undefined

21. An _____ or member of a set is an object that when collected together make up the set.
    a. Thing
    b. Element0
    c. Undefined
    d. Undefined

22. In mathematics, the _____ , or members of a set or more generally a class are all those objects which when collected together make up the set or class.
    a. Elements0
    b. Thing
    c. Undefined
    d. Undefined

23. In computer science an _____ is a data structure that consists of a group of elements having a single name that are accessed by indexing. In most programming languages each element has the same data type and the _____ occupies a continuous area of storage.
    a. Array0
    b. Thing
    c. Undefined
    d. Undefined

24. In mathematics, a _____ is a rectangular table of numbers or, more generally, a table consisting of abstract quantities that can be added and multiplied.
    a. Thing
    b. Matrix0
    c. Undefined
    d. Undefined

25. In physics and in _____ calculus, a spatial _____, or simply _____, is a concept characterized by a magnitude and a direction.
    a. Thing
    b. Vector0
    c. Undefined
    d. Undefined

26. In mathematics, a matrix can be thought of as each row or _____ being a vector. Hence, a space formed by row vectors or _____ vectors are said to be a row space or a _____ space.
    a. Concept
    b. Column0
    c. Undefined
    d. Undefined

27. _____ is an m × 1 matrix, i.e. a matrix consisting of a single column of m elements.
    a. Column vector0
    b. Thing
    c. Undefined
    d. Undefined

28. In linear algebra, a _____ is a 1 × n matrix, that is, a matrix consisting of a single row
    a. Row vector0
    b. Thing
    c. Undefined
    d. Undefined

29. In plane geometry, a _____ is a polygon with four equal sides, four right angles, and parallel opposite sides. In algebra, the _____ of a number is that number multiplied by itself.

Chapter 9. LINEAR ALCEBRA AND ANALYTIC GEOMETRY

  a. Square0
  c. Undefined
  b. Thing
  d. Undefined

30. A _____ can refer to a line joining two nonadjacent vertices of a polygon or polyhedron, or in some contexts any upward or downward sloping line. .
  a. Diagonal0
  b. Thing
  c. Undefined
  d. Undefined

31. In linear algebra, the _____ of a matrix is obtained by combining two matrices in such a way that a matrix of coefficients to which has been added a column of constants corresponds to the right hand side of the equations.
  a. Augmented matrix0
  b. Thing
  c. Undefined
  d. Undefined

32. In mathematics and more specifically set theory, the _____ set is the unique set which contains no elements.
  a. Thing
  b. Empty0
  c. Undefined
  d. Undefined

33. A _____ is a set of possible values that a variable can take on in order to satisfy a given set of conditions, which may include equations and inequalities.
  a. Solution set0
  b. Thing
  c. Undefined
  d. Undefined

34. A _____ is a set of numbers that designate location in a given reference system, such as x,y in a planar _____ system or an x,y,z in a three-dimensional _____ system.
  a. Thing
  b. Coordinate0
  c. Undefined
  d. Undefined

35. In mathematics and its applications, a _____ is a system for assigning an n-tuple of numbers or scalars to each point in an n-dimensional space.
  a. Concept
  b. Coordinate system0
  c. Undefined
  d. Undefined

36. In chemistry, a _____ is substance made by combining two or more different materials in such a way that no chemical reaction occurs.
  a. Thing
  b. Mixture0
  c. Undefined
  d. Undefined

37. In a mathematical proof or a syllogism, a _____ is a statement that is the logical consequence of preceding statements.
  a. Concept
  b. Conclusion0
  c. Undefined
  d. Undefined

38. In linear algebra, the _____ of a matrix A is another matrix AT
  a. Thing
  b. Transpose0
  c. Undefined
  d. Undefined

Chapter 9. LINEAR ALCEBRA AND ANALYTIC GEOMETRY

39. A _____ is a negotiable instrument instructing a financial institution to pay a specific amount of a specific currency from a specific demand account held in the maker/depositor's name with that institution. Both the maker and payee may be natural persons or legal entities.
   a. Thing
   b. Check0
   c. Undefined
   d. Undefined

40. In mathematics, _____ is an elementary arithmetic operation. When one of the numbers is a whole number, _____ is the repeated sum of the other number.
   a. Thing
   b. Multiplication0
   c. Undefined
   d. Undefined

41. _____ has many meanings, most of which simply .
   a. Thing
   b. Power0
   c. Undefined
   d. Undefined

42. An _____ is an equality that remains true regardless of the values of any variables that appear within it, to distinguish it from an equality which is true under more particular conditions.
   a. Identity0
   b. Thing
   c. Undefined
   d. Undefined

43. In mathematics, a _____ may be described informally as a number that can be given by an infinite decimal representation.
   a. Real number0
   b. Thing
   c. Undefined
   d. Undefined

44. In mathematics, a _____ is the result of multiplying, or an expression that identifies factors to be multiplied.
   a. Thing
   b. Product0
   c. Undefined
   d. Undcfincd

45. _____ element of an element x with respect to a binary operation * with identity element e is an element y such that x * y = y * x = e. In particular,
   a. Inverse0
   b. Thing
   c. Undefined
   d. Undefined

46. In mathematics, the multiplicative inverse of a number x, denoted 1/x or x^{-1}, is the number which, when multiplied by x, yields 1. The multiplicative inverse of x is also called the _____ of x.
   a. Thing
   b. Reciprocal0
   c. Undefined
   d. Undefined

47. In mathematics, the idea of _____ generalises the concepts of negation, in relation to addition, and reciprocal, in relation to multiplication.
   a. Inverse element0
   b. Thing
   c. Undefined
   d. Undefined

48. In common philosophical language, a proposition or _____, is the content of an assertion, that is, it is true-or-false and defined by the meaning of a particular piece of language.

a. Concept
b. Statement0
c. Undefined
d. Undefined

49. In linear algebra, the _____ refers to a matrix consisting of the coefficients of the variables in a set of linear equations.
   a. Thing
   b. Coefficient matrix0
   c. Undefined
   d. Undefined

50. In algebra, a _____ is a function depending on n that associates a scalar, $\det(A)$, to every $n \times n$ square matrix A.
   a. Thing
   b. Determinant0
   c. Undefined
   d. Undefined

51. In mathematics, a _____ in elementary terms is any of a variety of different functions from geometry, such as rotations, reflections and translations.
   a. Thing
   b. Transformation0
   c. Undefined
   d. Undefined

52. A _____ is 360° or 2δ radians.
   a. Turn0
   b. Thing
   c. Undefined
   d. Undefined

53. In sociology and biology a _____ is the collection of people or organisms of a particular species living in a given geographic area or space, usually measured by a census.
   a. Population0
   b. Thing
   c. Undefined
   d. Undefined

54. The word _____ comes from the 15th Century Latin word discretus which means separate.
   a. Thing
   b. Discrete0
   c. Undefined
   d. Undefined

55. _____ or life assurance is a contract between the policy owner and the insurer, where the insurer agrees to pay a sum of money upon the occurrence of the policy owner's death.
   a. Thing
   b. Life insurance0
   c. Undefined
   d. Undefined

56. _____, in law and economics, is a form of risk management primarily used to hedge against the risk of a contingent loss.
   a. Insurance0
   b. Thing
   c. Undefined
   d. Undefined

57. In set theory and its applications throughout mathematics, _____ are a collection of sets (or sometimes other mathematical objects) that can be unambiguously defined by a property that all its members share.
   a. Classes0
   b. Thing
   c. Undefined
   d. Undefined

58. _____ is the chance that something is likely to happen or be the case.

Chapter 9. LINEAR ALCEBRA AND ANALYTIC GEOMETRY

a. Probability0
b. Thing
c. Undefined
d. Undefined

59. In mathematical analysis, _____ are objects which generalize functions and probability distributions.
    a. Thing
    b. Distribution0
    c. Undefined
    d. Undefined

60. A vector can be thought of as an arrow. It has a length, called its magnitude, and it points in some particular direction. A linear transformation inputs a vector and changes it, usually changing both its magnitude and its direction. An eigenvector of a given linear transformation is a vector which is simply multiplied by a constant called the _____ during that transformation.
    a. Eigenvalue0
    b. Thing
    c. Undefined
    d. Undefined

61. An _____ of a linear transformation is a non-zero vector that is either left unaffected or simply multiplied by a scale factor after the transformation.
    a. Eigenvector0
    b. Thing
    c. Undefined
    d. Undefined

62. A _____ is the quantity that defines certain relatively constant characteristics of systems or functions..
    a. Thing
    b. Parameter0
    c. Undefined
    d. Undefined

63. In mathematics, a _____ is a two-dimensional manifold or surface that is perfectly flat.
    a. Plane0
    b. Thing
    c. Undefined
    d. Undefined

64. In mathematics, in the field of group theory, a _____ of a group is a quasisimple subnormal subgroup.
    a. Component0
    b. Concept
    c. Undefined
    d. Undefined

65. A _____, is a symbolized depiction of space which highlights relations between components of that space. Most usually a _____ is a two-dimensional, geometrically accurate representation of a three-dimensional space.
    a. Thing
    b. Map0
    c. Undefined
    d. Undefined

66. _____ means of or relating to the French philosopher and mathematician René Descartes.
    a. Cartesian0
    b. Thing
    c. Undefined
    d. Undefined

67. A _____ is the result of the addition of a set of numbers. The numbers may be natural numbers, complex numbers, matrices, or still more complicated objects. An infinite _____ is a subtle procedure known as a series.
    a. Thing
    b. Sum0
    c. Undefined
    d. Undefined

68. A _____ is a four-sided plane figure that has two sets of opposite parallel sides.

Chapter 9. LINEAR ALCEBRA AND ANALYTIC GEOMETRY

a. Concept
b. Parallelogram0
c. Undefined
d. Undefined

69. In linear algebra, real numbers are called scalars and relate to vectors in a vector space through the operation of _____ multiplication, in which a vector can be multiplied by a number to produce another vector.
a. Scalar0
b. Thing
c. Undefined
d. Undefined

70. In linear algebra and related areas of mathematics, the null vector or _____ is the vector in Euclidean space, all of whose components are zero.
a. Zero vector0
b. Thing
c. Undefined
d. Undefined

71. A _____ of a number is the product of that number with any integer.
a. Multiple0
b. Thing
c. Undefined
d. Undefined

72. In mathematics, _____ expressions is used to reduce the expression into the lowest possible term.
a. Thing
b. Simplifying0
c. Undefined
d. Undefined

73. A _____ is a movement of an object in a circular motion. A two-dimensional object rotates around a center (or point) of _____. A three-dimensional object rotates around a line called an axis. If the axis of _____ is within the body, the body is said to rotate upon itself, or spin—which implies relative speed and perhaps free-movement with angular momentum. A circular motion about an external point, e.g. the Earth about the Sun, is called an orbit or more properly an orbital revolution.
a. Rotation0
b. Thing
c. Undefined
d. Undefined

74. In mathematics, the _____ of a complex number z, is the first element of the ordered pair of real numbers representing z, i.e. if z = (x,y), or equivalently, z = x + iy, then the _____ of z is x. It is denoted by Re{z}. The complex function which maps z to the _____ of z is not holomorphic.
a. Real part0
b. Thing
c. Undefined
d. Undefined

75. In algebra, a _____ is a binomial formed by taking the opposite of the second term of a binomial.
a. Thing
b. Conjugate0
c. Undefined
d. Undefined

76. In linear algebra, the _____ of an n-by-n square matrix A is defined to be the sum of the elements on the main diagonal of A,
a. Thing
b. Trace0
c. Undefined
d. Undefined

77. In mathematics, a _____ is a statement that can be proved on the basis of explicitly stated or previously agreed assumptions.

Chapter 9. LINEAR ALCEBRA AND ANALYTIC GEOMETRY

a. Thing
c. Undefined
b. Theorem0
d. Undefined

78. In combinatorial mathematics, a _____ is an un-ordered collection of unique elements.
a. Combination0
c. Undefined
b. Concept
d. Undefined

79. _____ is a special mathematical relationship between two quantities. Two quantities are called proportional if they vary in such a way that one of the quantities is a constant multiple of the other, or equivalently if they have a constant ratio.
a. Proportionality0
c. Undefined
b. Thing
d. Undefined

80. In mathematics and logic, a _____ proof is a way of showing the truth or falsehood of a given statement by a straightforward combination of established facts, usually existing lemmas and theorems, without making any further assumptions.
a. Thing
c. Undefined
b. Direct0
d. Undefined

81. In functional analysis and related areas of mathematics the _____ set of a given subset of a vector space is a certain set in the dual space.
a. Thing
c. Undefined
b. Polar0
d. Undefined

82. _____ is the study of geometry using the principles of algebra. _____ can be explained more simply: it is concerned with defining geometrical shapes in a numerical way and extracting numerical information from that representation.
a. Thing
c. Undefined
b. Analytic geometry0
d. Undefined

83. _____ was a French lawyer and a mathematician who is given credit for early developments that led to modern calculus. In particular, he is recognized for his discovery of an original method of finding the greatest and the smallest ordinates of curved lines, which is analogous to that of the then unknown differential calculus.
a. Person
c. Undefined
b. Pierre de Fermat0
d. Undefined

84. _____ is a mathematical subject that includes the study of limits, derivatives, integrals, and power series and constitutes a major part of modern university curriculum.
a. Thing
c. Undefined
b. Calculus0
d. Undefined

85. _____ was a highly influential French philosopher, mathematician, scientist, and writer. Dubbed the "Founder of Modern Philosophy", and the "Father of Modern Mathematics". His theories provided the basis for the calculus of Newton and Leibniz, by applying infinitesimal calculus to the tangent line problem, thus permitting the evolution of that branch of modern mathematics

Chapter 9. LINEAR ALCEBRA AND ANALYTIC GEOMETRY

a. Descartes0
b. Person
c. Undefined
d. Undefined

86. An _____ is when two lines intersect somewhere on a plane creating a right angle at intersection
    a. Axes0
    b. Thing
    c. Undefined
    d. Undefined

87. In geometry, two lines or planes if one falls on the other in such a way as to create congruent adjacent angles. The term may be used as a noun or adjective. Thus, referring to Figure 1, the line AB is the _____ to CD through the point B.
    a. Thing
    b. Perpendicular0
    c. Undefined
    d. Undefined

88. In mathematics, the _____ is used to determine each point uniquely in a plane through two numbers, usually called the x-coordinate and the y-coordinate of the point.
    a. Thing
    b. Cartesian coordinate system0
    c. Undefined
    d. Undefined

89. _____ is a set, with some particular properties and usually some additional structure, such as the operations of addition or multiplication, for instance.
    a. Thing
    b. Space0
    c. Undefined
    d. Undefined

90. In geometry, a line _____ is a part of a line that is bounded by two end points, and contains every point on the line between its end points.
    a. Concept
    b. Segment0
    c. Undefined
    d. Undefined

91. Initial objects are also called _____, and terminal objects are also called final.
    a. Thing
    b. Coterminal0
    c. Undefined
    d. Undefined

92. In geometry, an _____ is a point at which a line segment or ray terminates.
    a. Endpoint0
    b. Thing
    c. Undefined
    d. Undefined

93. In mathematics, the _____ of a coordinate system is the point where the axes of the system intersect.
    a. Thing
    b. Origin0
    c. Undefined
    d. Undefined

94. A _____ is a part of a line that is bounded by two end points, and contains every point on the line between its end points.
    a. Line segment0
    b. Thing
    c. Undefined
    d. Undefined

95. In mathematics, a _____ number (or a _____) is a natural number that has exactly two (distinct) natural number divisors, which are 1 and the _____ number itself.

Chapter 9. LINEAR ALCEBRA AND ANALYTIC GEOMETRY

a. Thing
c. Undefined
b. Prime0
d. Undefined

96. In mathematics, the _____, also known as the scalar product, is a binary operation which takes two vectors over the real numbers R and returns a real-valued scalar quantity. It is the standard inner product of the Euclidean space.
a. Dot product0
c. Undefined
b. Thing
d. Undefined

97. _____ statistics are statistics that estimate population parameters.
a. Thing
c. Undefined
b. Parametric0
d. Undefined

98. In mathematics, _____ bear slight similarity to functions: they allow one to use arbitrary values, called parameters, in place of independent variables in equations, which in turn provide values for dependent variables. A simple kinematical example is when one uses a time parameter to determine the position, velocity, and other information about a body in motion.
a. Thing
c. Undefined
b. Parametric equations0
d. Undefined

99. _____ is a branch of mathematics which deals with triangles, particularly triangles in a plane where one angle of the triangle is 90 degrees, and a variety of other topological relations such as spheres, in other branches, such as spherical _____.
a. Thing
c. Undefined
b. Trigonometry0
d. Undefined

100. In geometry, a _____ is a special kind of point, usually a corner of a polygon, polyhedron, or higher dimensional polytope. In the geometry of curves a _____ is a point of where the first derivative of curvature is zero. In graph theory, a _____ is the fundamental unit out of which graphs are formed
a. Vertex0
c. Undefined
b. Thing
d. Undefined

101. The _____ is a unit of plane angle. It is represented by the symbol "rad" or, more rarely, by the superscript c (for "circular measure"). For example, an angle of 1.2 radians would be written "1.2 rad" or "1.2c" (second symbol can produce confusion with centigrads).
a. Radian0
c. Undefined
b. Thing
d. Undefined

102. In mathematics, there are several meanings of _____ depending on the subject.
a. Degree0
c. Undefined
b. Thing
d. Undefined

103. A _____ is a special kind of ratio, indicating a relationship between two measurements with different units, such as miles to gallons or cents to pounds.
a. Rate0
c. Undefined
b. Thing
d. Undefined

Chapter 10. MULTIVARIABLE CALCULUS

1. By _____ we mean collecting observations made upon our environment -- observations, which are the results of measurements using clocks, balances, measuring rods, counting operations, or other objectively defined measuring instruments or procedures. _____ may mean simply counting the number of times a particular property occurs.
   a. 15 theorem
   b. Data1
   c. Undefined
   d. Undefined

2. _____ are characteristics or properties of an object that can take on one or more different values.
   a. Variables1
   b. 15 theorem
   c. Undefined
   d. Undefined

3. _____ are those factors controlled by the experimenter.
   a. Independent variables1
   b. ACTRAN
   c. Undefined
   d. Undefined

4. The very fact that we are measuring objects with respect to some characteristic implies that the objects differ in that characteristic; or stated in another way, that the characteristic can take on a number of different values. These properties or characteristics of an object that can assume two or more different values are referred to as a _____.
   a. 15 theorem
   b. Variable1
   c. Undefined
   d. Undefined

5. In a large distribution of data it is often easier to understand the data if it is grouped into intervals where each _____ can contain more than one data value. Distributions are often reduced to 10 to 20 intervals.
   a. ACTRAN
   b. Interval1
   c. Undefined
   d. Undefined

6. A measure of variability, the _____ is the distance from the lowest to the highest score.
   a. Range1
   b. 15 theorem
   c. Undefined
   d. Undefined

7. In inferential statistics where we are using a statistic to infer differences we need at least two different variables typically called an _____ and a dependent variable. The _____ represents the variable of interest, that is, the variable in which an inference is being made as to whether categories of that variable should be considered the same or different. There must be at least two categories or groupings for this variable in order to make comparisons. The variable is said to be independent since the categories are arbitrarily assigned by the investigator.
   a. ACTRAN
   b. Independent variable1
   c. Undefined
   d. Undefined

8. A number that does not change in value in a given situation is a _____.
   a. Constant1
   b. 15 theorem
   c. Undefined
   d. Undefined

9. By _____ we mean the cumulative frequency, counting in from the nearer end.
   a. 15 theorem
   b. Depth1
   c. Undefined
   d. Undefined

Chapter 10. MULTIVARIABLE CALCULUS

10. A _____ is a subset or portion of a population. Samples are extremely important in the field of statistical analysis, since due to economic and practical constraints we usually cannot make measurements on every single member of the particular population.
    a. 15 theorem
    b. Sample1
    c. Undefined
    d. Undefined

11. A population, also referred to as a universe, is any well-defined collection of things. By well-defined we mean that the members of the _____ are spelled out, or an unequivocal statement is made as to which things belong in it and which do not.
    a. 15 theorem
    b. Population1
    c. Undefined
    d. Undefined

12. The _____ is a result used to determine the probability that event A or event B occurs or both occur.
    a. Addition Rule1
    b. ACTRAN
    c. Undefined
    d. Undefined

13. _____ is used synonymously for variable.
    a. 15 theorem
    b. Factor1
    c. Undefined
    d. Undefined

14. The _____ is a result used to determine the probability that two events, A and B, both occur.
    a. 15 theorem
    b. Multiplication Rule1
    c. Undefined
    d. Undefined

15. At times we must contend with variables that assume a large number of values. In this case it is typical to create _____ of values of the variable and then make a frequency tally of the number of observations falling within each interval. As is the case with any data reduction technique, detail is lost.
    a. ACTRAN
    b. Intervals1
    c. Undefined
    d. Undefined

16. An _____ is any process or study, which results in the collection of data, the outcome of which is unknown. In statistics, the term is usually restricted to situations in which the researcher has control over some of the conditions under which the _____ takes place.
    a. ACTRAN
    b. Experiment1
    c. Undefined
    d. Undefined

17. We are concerned with the analysis of data generated from an experiment. It is wise to take time and effort to organize the experiment properly to ensure that the right type of data, and enough of it, is available to answer the questions of interest as clearly and efficiently as possible. This process is called _____.
    a. Experimental Design1
    b. ACTRAN
    c. Undefined
    d. Undefined

18. The _____ refers to the amount of change in Y for a 1 unit change in X; or in-other-words, the rate of change in the predicted value as a function of a change in the predictor variable.

a. Slope1
b. 15 theorem
c. Undefined
d. Undefined

19. _____, the height of the curve for a given value of X; closely related to the probability of an observation in an interval around X.
a. Density1
b. 15 theorem
c. Undefined
d. Undefined

20. There are properties of objects that do assume one and only value, and we refer to these characteristics as constants. _____, then, are the invariables that differentiate one class of objects from another.
a. 15 theorem
b. Constants1
c. Undefined
d. Undefined

21. Another word for independent variables in the analysis of variance is _____.
a. 15 theorem
b. Factors1
c. Undefined
d. Undefined

22. The most important measure of central tendency, and one of the basic building blocks of all statistical analysis, is the arithmetic _____. It is simply the sum of all the set of values divided by the number of values involved. As a measure of central tendency, it is affected by extreme scores, and it assumes a ratio scale of measurement.
a. Mean1
b. 15 theorem
c. Undefined
d. Undefined

23. A _____ is a value used to represent a certain population characteristic. Because of the impracticality of measuring an entire population to determine this value, parameters are usually estimated.
a. 15 theorem
b. Parameter1
c. Undefined
d. Undefined

24. A common requirement for parametric tests is that the population of scores from which the sample observations came should be normally distributed. While many variables are close enough to a normal distribution and many of the tests that we will encounter are quite robust to moderate departures, occasionally there is a need to transform a variable so that the requirement of normality is better met; called _____. Essentially this means transforming the distribution such that the symmetry of the distribution is made to resemble a normal distribution more closely.
a. 15 theorem
b. Normalizing1
c. Undefined
d. Undefined

25. A _____ provides a quantitative description of the likely occurrence of a particular event. _____ is conventionally expressed on a scale from 0 to 1; a rare event has a _____ close to 0, a very common event has a _____ close to 1. _____ is calculated as the ratio of the number of favorable events to the total number of possible events.
a. 15 theorem
b. Probability1
c. Undefined
d. Undefined

26. The number of times a particular score or event occurs with respect to the total number of events or scores is called its _____.

Chapter 10. MULTIVARIABLE CALCULUS

a. 15 theorem
c. Undefined
b. Proportion1
d. Undefined

27. The defining characteristics of populations are called _____. Observations must be made on every single member of the population in question in order to precisely state the value of _____.
a. Parameters1
c. Undefined
b. 15 theorem
d. Undefined

28. A _____ is a scheme for the numerical representation of the values of a variable. The interpretation we place upon the numbers of the scale, rather than the numbers themselves, makes the _____ useful. The most common scales are nominal, ordinal, interval
a. 15 theorem
c. Undefined
b. Scale1
d. Undefined

29. A _____ is simply a polynomial with two terms.
a. Binomial1
c. Undefined
b. 15 theorem
d. Undefined

30. Horizontal axis of display containing the trailing digits is called _____.
a. 15 theorem
c. Undefined
b. Leaves1
d. Undefined

Chapter 11. SYSTEMS OF DIFFFRENTIAL EQUATIONS

1. In inferential statistics where we are using a statistic to infer differences we need at least two different variables typically called an _____ and a dependent variable. The _____ represents the variable of interest, that is, the variable in which an inference is being made as to whether categories of that variable should be considered the same or different. There must be at least two categories or groupings for this variable in order to make comparisons. The variable is said to be independent since the categories are arbitrarily assigned by the investigator.
   a. Independent variable1
   b. ACTRAN
   c. Undefined
   d. Undefined

2. The very fact that we are measuring objects with respect to some characteristic implies that the objects differ in that characteristic; or stated in another way, that the characteristic can take on a number of different values. These properties or characteristics of an object that can assume two or more different values are referred to as a _____.
   a. 15 theorem
   b. Variable1
   c. Undefined
   d. Undefined

3. _____ are characteristics or properties of an object that can take on one or more different values.
   a. 15 theorem
   b. Variables1
   c. Undefined
   d. Undefined

4. A number that does not change in value in a given situation is a _____.
   a. 15 theorem
   b. Constant1
   c. Undefined
   d. Undefined

5. The defining characteristics of populations are called _____. Observations must be made on every single member of the population in question in order to precisely state the value of _____.
   a. 15 theorem
   b. Parameters1
   c. Undefined
   d. Undefined

6. There are properties of objects that do assume one and only value, and we refer to these characteristics as constants. _____, then, are the invariables that differentiate one class of objects from another.
   a. Constants1
   b. 15 theorem
   c. Undefined
   d. Undefined

7. The _____ refers to the amount of change in Y for a 1 unit change in X; or in-other-words, the rate of change in the predicted value as a function of a change in the predictor variable.
   a. Slope1
   b. 15 theorem
   c. Undefined
   d. Undefined

8. A _____ is a scheme for the numerical representation of the values of a variable. The interpretation we place upon the numbers of the scale, rather than the numbers themselves, makes the _____ useful. The most common scales are nominal, ordinal, interval
   a. Scale1
   b. 15 theorem
   c. Undefined
   d. Undefined

9. The most important measure of central tendency, and one of the basic building blocks of all statistical analysis, is the arithmetic _____. It is simply the sum of all the set of values divided by the number of values involved. As a measure of central tendency, it is affected by extreme scores, and it assumes a ratio scale of measurement.

Chapter 11. SYSTEMS OF DIFFRENTIAL EQUATIONS

a. 15 theorem
b. Mean1
c. Undefined
d. Undefined

10. A _____ is a value used to represent a certain population characteristic. Because of the impracticality of measuring an entire population to determine this value, parameters are usually estimated.
a. Parameter1
b. 15 theorem
c. Undefined
d. Undefined

11. In a factorial design with two or more main effects or grouping effects, there is a possibility of a significant _____ effect, AB. With a significant _____ you have differences in estimates of the population variance in the various combinations, or cells, of one main effect paired with another. Interactions must be explained before main effects in a statistical analysis. The _____ is tested using an F test in an ANOVA that compares the MSab/Mserror.
a. ACTRAN
b. Interaction1
c. Undefined
d. Undefined

12. A population, also referred to as a universe, is any well-defined collection of things. By well-defined we mean that the members of the _____ are spelled out, or an unequivocal statement is made as to which things belong in it and which do not.
a. 15 theorem
b. Population1
c. Undefined
d. Undefined

13. An _____ is the result of an experiment or other situation involving uncertainty.
a. ACTRAN
b. Outcome1
c. Undefined
d. Undefined

14. By _____ we mean collecting observations made upon our environment -- observations, which are the results of measurements using clocks, balances, measuring rods, counting operations, or other objectively defined measuring instruments or procedures. _____ may mean simply counting the number of times a particular property occurs.
a. Data1
b. 15 theorem
c. Undefined
d. Undefined

15. A _____ refers to the distance or difference between any score in a distribution of data from the mean.
a. 15 theorem
b. Deviation1
c. Undefined
d. Undefined

16. Another word for independent variables in the analysis of variance is _____.
a. Factors1
b. 15 theorem
c. Undefined
d. Undefined

17. _____, the height of the curve for a given value of X; closely related to the probability of an observation in an interval around X.
a. Density1
b. 15 theorem
c. Undefined
d. Undefined

18. The combination of a particular row and column; the set of observations obtained under identical treatment conditions is simply a _____.

a. Cell1
b. 15 theorem
c. Undefined
d. Undefined

19. _____ is used synonymously for variable.
    a. 15 theorem
    b. Factor1
    c. Undefined
    d. Undefined

20. Horizontal axis of display containing the trailing digits is called _____.
    a. 15 theorem
    b. Leaves1
    c. Undefined
    d. Undefined

Chapter 12. PROBABILITY AND STATISTICS

1. A _____ provides a quantitative description of the likely occurrence of a particular event. _____ is conventionally expressed on a scale from 0 to 1; a rare event has a _____ close to 0, a very common event has a _____ close to 1. _____ is calculated as the ratio of the number of favorable events to the total number of possible events.
   - a. 15 theorem
   - b. Probability1
   - c. Undefined
   - d. Undefined

2. Statistical analysis, sometimes referred to simply as _____, is concerned with the definition and collection, organization, and interpretation of data according to well-defined procedures. The term itself, _____, is a defining characteristic of a sample, such as a sample mean, or sample standard deviation.
   - a. 15 theorem
   - b. Statistics1
   - c. Undefined
   - d. Undefined

3. By _____ we mean collecting observations made upon our environment -- observations, which are the results of measurements using clocks, balances, measuring rods, counting operations, or other objectively defined measuring instruments or procedures. _____ may mean simply counting the number of times a particular property occurs.
   - a. 15 theorem
   - b. Data1
   - c. Undefined
   - d. Undefined

4. In experiments, a _____ is something that researchers administer to experimental units.
   - a. 15 theorem
   - b. Treatment1
   - c. Undefined
   - d. Undefined

5. An _____ is any process or study, which results in the collection of data, the outcome of which is unknown. In statistics, the term is usually restricted to situations in which the researcher has control over some of the conditions under which the _____ takes place.
   - a. Experiment1
   - b. ACTRAN
   - c. Undefined
   - d. Undefined

6. _____ refer to any data source, whether individuals, physical or biological things, geographic locations, time periods, or events; that is, anything upon which observations can be made.
   - a. Objects1
   - b. ACTRAN
   - c. Undefined
   - d. Undefined

7. Another word for independent variables in the analysis of variance is _____.
   - a. 15 theorem
   - b. Factors1
   - c. Undefined
   - d. Undefined

8. _____ is used synonymously for variable.
   - a. Factor1
   - b. 15 theorem
   - c. Undefined
   - d. Undefined

9. A _____ is simply a polynomial with two terms.
   - a. 15 theorem
   - b. Binomial1
   - c. Undefined
   - d. Undefined

10. A _____ is an inactive treatment or procedure. It literally means 'I do nothing'. The _____ effect' (usually a positive or beneficial response) is attributable to the patient's expectation that the treatment will have an effect.
   a. 15 theorem
   b. Placebo1
   c. Undefined
   d. Undefined

11. The same statistical principles apply to the evaluation of observed _____ between sets of data. The field of statistics provides the necessary techniques for making statements of our certainty that there are real as opposed to chance differences.
   a. 15 theorem
   b. Differences1
   c. Undefined
   d. Undefined

12. A _____ is a subset or portion of a population. Samples are extremely important in the field of statistical analysis, since due to economic and practical constraints we usually cannot make measurements on every single member of the particular population.
   a. 15 theorem
   b. Sample1
   c. Undefined
   d. Undefined

13. An _____ is the result of an experiment or other situation involving uncertainty.
   a. ACTRAN
   b. Outcome1
   c. Undefined
   d. Undefined

14. The _____ is an exhaustive list of all the possible outcomes of an experiment. Each possible result of such a study is represented by one and only one point in the sample space, which is usually denoted by S.
   a. Sample Space1
   b. 15 theorem
   c. Undefined
   d. Undefined

15. A population, also referred to as a universe, is any well-defined collection of things. By well-defined we mean that the members of the _____ are spelled out, or an unequivocal statement is made as to which things belong in it and which do not.
   a. Population1
   b. 15 theorem
   c. Undefined
   d. Undefined

16. _____ refers to the process of selecting one or more samples of a population. Samples may be selected randomly or systematically.
   a. Sampling1
   b. 15 theorem
   c. Undefined
   d. Undefined

17. The outcome of a trial is called the _____.
   a. ACTRAN
   b. Event1
   c. Undefined
   d. Undefined

18. The _____ is a result used to determine the probability that two events, A and B, both occur.
   a. 15 theorem
   b. Multiplication Rule1
   c. Undefined
   d. Undefined

Chapter 12. PROBABILITY AND STATISTICS

19. An _____ is an indication of the value of an unknown quantity based on observed data. More formally, an _____ is the particular value of an estimator that is obtained from a particular sample of data and used to indicate the value of a parameter.
    a. Estimate1
    b. ACTRAN
    c. Undefined
    d. Undefined

20. The probability of one event given the occurrence of some other event is a _____.
    a. 15 theorem
    b. Conditional probability1
    c. Undefined
    d. Undefined

21. The number of times a particular score or event occurs with respect to the total number of events or scores is called its _____.
    a. 15 theorem
    b. Proportion1
    c. Undefined
    d. Undefined

22. The probability of one event ignoring the occurrence or nonoccurrence of some other event is _____.
    a. Unconditional probability1
    b. ACTRAN
    c. Undefined
    d. Undefined

23. The very fact that we are measuring objects with respect to some characteristic implies that the objects differ in that characteristic; or stated in another way, that the characteristic can take on a number of different values. These properties or characteristics of an object that can assume two or more different values are referred to as a _____.
    a. 15 theorem
    b. Variable1
    c. Undefined
    d. Undefined

24. One major objective of statistical analysis is the identification of associations or _____ that exist between and among sets of observations. In other words, does knowledge about about one set of data allow us to infer or predict characteristics about another set or sets of data.
    a. Relationships1
    b. 15 theorem
    c. Undefined
    d. Undefined

25. _____ are characteristics or properties of an object that can take on one or more different values.
    a. Variables1
    b. 15 theorem
    c. Undefined
    d. Undefined

26. The outcome of an experiment need not be a number, for example, the outcome when a coin is tossed can be 'heads' or 'tails'. However, we often want to represent outcomes as numbers. A _____ is a function that associates a unique numerical value with every outcome of an experiment. The value of the random
    a. Random Variable1
    b. 15 theorem
    c. Undefined
    d. Undefined

27. A measure of variability, the _____ is the distance from the lowest to the highest score.
    a. Range1
    b. 15 theorem
    c. Undefined
    d. Undefined

Chapter 12. PROBABILITY AND STATISTICS

28. A _____ is one which may take on only a countable number of distinct values such as 0,1,2,3,4,........ Discrete random variables are usually (but not necessarily) counts. If a random variable can take only a finite number of distinct values, then it must be discrete. Examples of discrete random variables include the number of children in a family, the Friday night attendance at a cinema, the number of patients in a doctor's surgery, the number of defective light bulbs in a box of ten.
   a. 15 theorem
   b. Discrete Random Variable1
   c. Undefined
   d. Undefined

29. A _____ is one, which takes an infinite number of possible values. Continuous random variables are usually measurements. Examples include height, weight, the amount of sugar in an orange, the time required to run a mile.
   a. 15 theorem
   b. Continuous Random Variable1
   c. Undefined
   d. Undefined

30. In statistics an arrangement of values of a variable showing their observed or theoretical frequency of occurrence is called a _____.
   a. 15 theorem
   b. Distribution1
   c. Undefined
   d. Undefined

31. The _____ provides the probability value associated with each point in a distribution of scores. The value indicates the likelihood of obtaining such a value from the distribution.
   a. Probability distribution1
   b. 15 theorem
   c. Undefined
   d. Undefined

32. A number that does not change in value in a given situation is a _____.
   a. 15 theorem
   b. Constant1
   c. Undefined
   d. Undefined

33. The most important measure of central tendency, and one of the basic building blocks of all statistical analysis, is the arithmetic _____. It is simply the sum of all the set of values divided by the number of values involved. As a measure of central tendency, it is affected by extreme scores, and it assumes a ratio scale of measurement.
   a. Mean1
   b. 15 theorem
   c. Undefined
   d. Undefined

34. The _____ is the a statistic which measures how spread out or dispersed a set of data is. It is The value calculated will always be greater than or equal to zero, with larger values corresponding to data which is more spread out. If all data values are identical, the _____ is equal to zero. The _____ is calculated as the mean square error: the sum of squared deviations about the mean, divided by the number of scores -1 degree of freedom.
   a. Variance1
   b. 15 theorem
   c. Undefined
   d. Undefined

35. The long-range average of a statistic over repeated samples is the _____.
   a. Expected value1
   b. ACTRAN
   c. Undefined
   d. Undefined

36. The number of times a particular score or observation occurs is its _____.

Chapter 12. PROBABILITY AND STATISTICS

a. Frequency1
b. 15 theorem
c. Undefined
d. Undefined

37. _____ is another term for proportion; it is the value calculated by dividing the number of times an event occurs by the total number of times an experiment is carried out. The probability of an event can be thought of as its long-run _____ when an experiment is carried out many times.
a. Relative frequency1
b. 15 theorem
c. Undefined
d. Undefined

38. It is often helpful to convert the frequencies of a frequency distribution into relative frequencies, which are the observed frequencies converted into percentages based on the total number of observations. The _____ tell us at a glance what percentage of the distribution had a particular value.
a. Relative frequencies1
b. 15 theorem
c. Undefined
d. Undefined

39. Horizontal axis of display containing the trailing digits is called _____.
a. 15 theorem
b. Leaves1
c. Undefined
d. Undefined

40. A simple tally or count of how often each value of a variable occurs among the set of measured objects is a frequency distribution. In constructing a _____, the most usual arrangement of the values of the variable is either from lowest to highest or highest to lowest. Frequency distributions are often graphed using histograms for categorical data, or polygons for quantitative data.
a. Frequency distribution1
b. 15 theorem
c. Undefined
d. Undefined

41. By _____ we mean an average calculated by taking into account not only the frequencies of the values of a variable but also some other factor such as their variance. The _____ of observed data is the result of dividing the sum of the products of each observed value, the number of times it occurs, and this other factor by the total number of observations
a. Weighted average1
b. 15 theorem
c. Undefined
d. Undefined

42. A measure of variability in a distribution, the _____ is the square root of the variance. The _____ measures the variability of scores around the mean: the standardized difference. It is the square root of the mean square error.
a. 15 theorem
b. Standard deviation1
c. Undefined
d. Undefined

43. A _____ refers to the distance or difference between any score in a distribution of data from the mean.
a. Deviation1
b. 15 theorem
c. Undefined
d. Undefined

44. A _____ involves the addition, subtraction, multiplication, or division of one variable by another variable or by a constant.

a. Linear transformation1
b. 15 theorem
c. Undefined
d. Undefined

45. There are properties of objects that do assume one and only value, and we refer to these characteristics as constants. _____, then, are the invariables that differentiate one class of objects from another.
   a. Constants1
   b. 15 theorem
   c. Undefined
   d. Undefined

46. The probability of the co-occurrence of two or more events is the _____.
   a. 15 theorem
   b. Joint probability1
   c. Undefined
   d. Undefined

47. _____ refers to two random variables X and Y, which are said to be independent if and only if the value of X has no influence on the value of Y and vice versa.
   a. ACTRAN
   b. Independent Random Variables1
   c. Undefined
   d. Undefined

48. The number of successes in n independent trials that each have the same probability p of success has the _____ with parameters n and p. For example, the number of heads in 10 tosses of a fair coin has a _____ with parameters n=10 and p=50%. The expected value of the _____ is n×p, and the standard error of the _____ is (n×p×(1-p))½.
   a. 15 theorem
   b. Binomial distribution1
   c. Undefined
   d. Undefined

49. The defining characteristics of populations are called _____. Observations must be made on every single member of the population in question in order to precisely state the value of _____.
   a. Parameters1
   b. 15 theorem
   c. Undefined
   d. Undefined

50. _____ is sampling in which the item drawn on trial N is replaced before the drawing on trial N+1.
   a. 15 theorem
   b. Sample with replacement1
   c. Undefined
   d. Undefined

51. _____, typically refers to a Geometric random variable that is the number of trials required to obtain the first failure.
   a. 15 theorem
   b. Geometric Distribution1
   c. Undefined
   d. Undefined

52. A _____ models discrete random variables. Typically, a Poisson random variable is a count of the number of events that occur in a certain time interval or spatial area.
   a. 15 theorem
   b. Poisson distribution1
   c. Undefined
   d. Undefined

53. A _____ is a value used to represent a certain population characteristic. Because of the impracticality of measuring an entire population to determine this value, parameters are usually estimated.

a. Parameter1
b. 15 theorem
c. Undefined
d. Undefined

54. _____, the height of the curve for a given value of X; closely related to the probability of an observation in an interval around X.
   a. 15 theorem
   b. Density1
   c. Undefined
   d. Undefined

55. In a large distribution of data it is often easier to understand the data if it is grouped into intervals where each _____ can contain more than one data value. Distributions are often reduced to 10 to 20 intervals.
   a. ACTRAN
   b. Interval1
   c. Undefined
   d. Undefined

56. At times we must contend with variables that assume a large number of values. In this case it is typical to create _____ of values of the variable and then make a frequency tally of the number of observations falling within each interval. As is the case with any data reduction technique, detail is lost.
   a. Intervals1
   b. ACTRAN
   c. Undefined
   d. Undefined

57. A _____, or bar chart, shows the values of the variable (or an interval of values) on the horizontal axis (abcissa or X-axis) and the heights of the bars above each value represents their frequencies of occurrence (the value on the ordinate or Y-axis).
   a. 15 theorem
   b. Histogram1
   c. Undefined
   d. Undefined

58. The _____ is often confused with the median. The Median is a statistic for the distribution whereas the _____ provides a statistic for an interval; it is the center of the interval; the arithmetic average of the upper and lower limits.
   a. 15 theorem
   b. Midpoint1
   c. Undefined
   d. Undefined

59. A property of a statistic whose long-range average is not equal to the parameter it estimates is called _____.
   a. Bias1
   b. 15 theorem
   c. Undefined
   d. Undefined

60. A _____ is a scheme for the numerical representation of the values of a variable. The interpretation we place upon the numbers of the scale, rather than the numbers themselves, makes the _____ useful. The most common scales are nominal, ordinal, interval
   a. 15 theorem
   b. Scale1
   c. Undefined
   d. Undefined

61. _____ is implied when data values are distributed in the same way above and below the middle of the sample.
   a. 15 theorem
   b. Symmetry1
   c. Undefined
   d. Undefined

62. According to the central limit theorem, the distribution of an average tends to be Normal, even when the distribution from which the average is computed is decidedly non-Normal. Thus, the _____ is the foundation for many statistical procedures, including Quality Control Charts, because the distribution of the phenomenon under study does not have to be Normal because it's average will be providing there is a large enough sample. The _____ specifies the nature of the sampling distribution of the mean.
   a. 15 theorem
   b. Central limit theorem1
   c. Undefined
   d. Undefined

63. _____ is the result of assigning numbers to objects to abstractly represent the objects or characteristics of the objects.
   a. 15 theorem
   b. Measurement1
   c. Undefined
   d. Undefined

64. _____ model refers to (some) continuous random variables and (some) discrete random variables. The values of a uniform random variable are uniformly distributed over an interval.
   a. Uniform Distribution1
   b. ACTRAN
   c. Undefined
   d. Undefined

65. The probability of correctly rejecting a false Ho is referred to as _____.
   a. 15 theorem
   b. Power1
   c. Undefined
   d. Undefined

66. A measure of central tendency, the median, corresponds to the point having 50% of the observations below it when observations are arranged in numerical order. The _____ assumes at least an interval level of measurement. For a symmetric distribution such as the normal distribution, the _____ is the same as the mean. For a distribution which is skewed to the right, the _____ is typically smaller than the mean or when skewed to the left, the _____ is smaller.
   a. 15 theorem
   b. Median1
   c. Undefined
   d. Undefined

67. By a _____ we mean that every member of a population has an equal chance of being included in the sample; more strictly, every possible sample of the specified size has an equal chance of being selected from the population.
   a. Random sample1
   b. 15 theorem
   c. Undefined
   d. Undefined

68. Whereas a defining characteristic of a population is referred to as a parameter, that characteristic when measured only on a sample is referred to as a _____. Statistics describe a characteristic of sample and since a sample is an estimate of a population, several statistics are used to estimate a parameter. The greater the number of samples and statistics taken, the better the estimate of the population and the parameter.
   a. 15 theorem
   b. Statistic1
   c. Undefined
   d. Undefined

69. The _____ is an estimator available for estimating the population mean. It is a measure of location, commonly called the average.
   a. 15 theorem
   b. Sample Mean1
   c. Undefined
   d. Undefined

Chapter 12. PROBABILITY AND STATISTICS

70. Sum of the squared deviations about the mean divided by N – 1 provides us the _____.
    a. Sample variance1
    b. 15 theorem
    c. Undefined
    d. Undefined

71. In statistics we use the deviations about the mean in many analyses to determine the amount of spread or distance among the scores to determine whether their is a significant enough difference to warrant saying that the values all describe the same object or whether they most likely describe different objects. Since we are interested in distance and not direction, we need the absolute values of the deviations. We use _____ which converts all numbers to positive values. Taking the square root of the result gives an absolute value.
    a. Squared deviations1
    b. 15 theorem
    c. Undefined
    d. Undefined

72. The _____ descrives the central tendency of a population rather than a sample. It is a parameter and not a statistic. Because of the difficulty in measuring the population mean, it is usually estimated from one or more samples.
    a. Population mean1
    b. 15 theorem
    c. Undefined
    d. Undefined

73. An _____ is any quantity calculated from the sample data, which is used to give information about an unknown quantity in the population.
    a. ACTRAN
    b. Estimator1
    c. Undefined
    d. Undefined

74. The _____ is usually estimated, rarely computed. To calculate the population variance, as any other parameter of a population, you must know every value in the population.
    a. 15 theorem
    b. Population variance1
    c. Undefined
    d. Undefined

75. _____ is the standard deviation of the values of a given function of the data (parameter), over all possible samples of the same size.
    a. Standard Error1
    b. 15 theorem
    c. Undefined
    d. Undefined

76. An interval, with limits at either end, with a specified probability of including the parameter being estimated is the _____.
    a. 15 theorem
    b. Confidence interval1
    c. Undefined
    d. Undefined

77. _____ in which the relationship between two or more variables is described as linear.
    a. 15 theorem
    b. Linear regression1
    c. Undefined
    d. Undefined

78. _____ describes the phenomenon where the values of distribution tend to move towards the summary statistic. For example, values in a distribution tend to cluster about the mean, and in a linear _____ equation, they tend to cluster about the linear _____ equation.

a. 15 theorem
c. Undefined
b. Regression1
d. Undefined

79. The method of _____ is a criterion for fitting a specified model to observed data.
    a. 15 theorem
    c. Undefined
    b. Least Squares1
    d. Undefined

80. The 'line of best fit' that represents a straight line drawn through the data points is the _____. .
    a. Regression line1
    c. Undefined
    b. 15 theorem
    d. Undefined

81. The _____ is a reoccurring calculation throughout much of statistic analysis. It is simply the sum of the squared deviations about the mean. When divided by N - 1 degree of freedom it provides us the variance or Mean Square error: SS / N-1. The square root of SS/N-1 provides the standard deviation.
    a. 15 theorem
    c. Undefined
    b. Sum of squares1
    d. Undefined

82. Students of statistics often confuse the terms variability and variance. The term 'Sums of Squares' is a short hand for the sum of the squared deviations about a statistic, such as the mean. Variability refers directly to the _____ for a variable, while variance refers to the _____ divided by the degrees of freedom or simply N-1. _____ are widely used because they are additive. Once we divide by N-1, the additive property disappears. Thus, Variance = SS / N-1.
    a. 15 theorem
    c. Undefined
    b. Sums of squares1
    d. Undefined

83. The _____ refers to the amount of change in Y for a 1 unit change in X; or in-other-words, the rate of change in the predicted value as a function of a change in the predictor variable.
    a. 15 theorem
    c. Undefined
    b. Slope1
    d. Undefined

84. The value of Y when X is 0 is the _____.
    a. Intercept1
    c. Undefined
    b. ACTRAN
    d. Undefined

85. The probability of a Type I error is referred to as _____.
    a. Alpha1
    c. Undefined
    b. ACTRAN
    d. Undefined

86. _____ is the probability of a Type II error
    a. 15 theorem
    c. Undefined
    b. Beta1
    d. Undefined

87. The symbol for the effect size is _____.
    a. 15 theorem
    c. Undefined
    b. Gamma1
    d. Undefined

88. The correlation coefficient when both of the variables are measured as dichotomies is _____.

a. Phi1
c. Undefined

b. 15 theorem
d. Undefined

89. The Greek letter _____ indicates summation.
a. Sigma1
c. Undefined

b. 15 theorem
d. Undefined

Chapter 1

1. a	2. a	3. b	4. b	5. a	6. b	7. a	8. a	9. a	10. b
11. b	12. b	13. b	14. a	15. b	16. a	17. b	18. b	19. b	20. a
21. a	22. b	23. a	24. a	25. a	26. b	27. b	28. b	29. a	30. b
31. a	32. b	33. b	34. a	35. b	36. b	37. b	38. b	39. a	40. b
41. b	42. a	43. b	44. a	45. a	46. a	47. b	48. a	49. b	50. b
51. b	52. a	53. a	54. b	55. a	56. a	57. a	58. b	59. a	60. b
61. b	62. b	63. a	64. a	65. b	66. b	67. a	68. a	69. b	70. b
71. b	72. b	73. a	74. a	75. a	76. b	77. b	78. b	79. b	80. b
81. a	82. a	83. a	84. b	85. b	86. b	87. b	88. b	89. b	90. a
91. b	92. b	93. a	94. b	95. a	96. a	97. b	98. b	99. a	100. b
101. b	102. a	103. b	104. a	105. a	106. b	107. b	108. b	109. b	110. b
111. b	112. a	113. b	114. b	115. a	116. b	117. b	118. b	119. a	120. a
121. b	122. b	123. a	124. b	125. b	126. b	127. a	128. a	129. b	130. b
131. a	132. b	133. b	134. b	135. b	136. a	137. b	138. a	139. a	140. b
141. b	142. a	143. a	144. a	145. a	146. b	147. a	148. b	149. a	150. a
151. a	152. a	153. a	154. b	155. a	156. a	157. a	158. a	159. b	160. b
161. b	162. a	163. b	164. a	165. a	166. a	167. b	168. b	169. a	170. b
171. b	172. a	173. b	174. a	175. b	176. a	177. a	178. a	179. a	180. b
181. a	182. b	183. b	184. b	185. b	186. a	187. b	188. a	189. a	190. b
191. b	192. a	193. b	194. b	195. a	196. a	197. a	198. b	199. a	200. b
201. a	202. a	203. b	204. b						

Chapter 2

1. b	2. b	3. b	4. b	5. b	6. b	7. b	8. b	9. b	10. b
11. b	12. b	13. a	14. b	15. b	16. a	17. a	18. a	19. a	20. a
21. a	22. b	23. b	24. a	25. a	26. b	27. a	28. a	29. b	30. a
31. a	32. b	33. a	34. a	35. b	36. b	37. a	38. b	39. b	40. a
41. a	42. b	43. a	44. b	45. b	46. b	47. b	48. a	49. a	50. a
51. b	52. a	53. a	54. b	55. a	56. a	57. a	58. b	59. b	60. b
61. a	62. b	63. b	64. b	65. a	66. a	67. a	68. a	69. a	70. a
71. b	72. a								

Chapter 3

1. b	2. a	3. a	4. a	5. a	6. a	7. a	8. a	9. a	10. b
11. b	12. a	13. a	14. b	15. a	16. a	17. b	18. b	19. b	20. b
21. a	22. b	23. a	24. a	25. a	26. b	27. a	28. b	29. b	30. b
31. b	32. a	33. b	34. b	35. b	36. a	37. a	38. a	39. a	40. b
41. a	42. a	43. b	44. b	45. a	46. b	47. b	48. a	49. b	50. a
51. a	52. a	53. a	54. b	55. b	56. b	57. b	58. b	59. a	60. a
61. b	62. a	63. b	64. a	65. b	66. b	67. b	68. b	69. a	70. a
71. b	72. a	73. b	74. b	75. a	76. a	77. a	78. b	79. a	80. b
81. a	82. b	83. b	84. a	85. a	86. b	87. b	88. b	89. a	90. a
91. b	92. b	93. a	94. b	95. a	96. b				

ANSWER KEY

Chapter 4

1. a	2. b	3. b	4. a	5. b	6. a	7. a	8. b	9. b	10. a
11. a	12. a	13. a	14. a	15. b	16. a	17. b	18. a	19. b	20. b
21. b	22. a	23. a	24. b	25. b	26. a	27. b	28. a	29. b	30. b
31. a	32. b	33. b	34. a	35. a	36. a	37. a	38. b	39. a	40. b
41. a	42. a	43. a	44. b	45. b	46. b	47. a	48. a	49. b	50. b
51. a	52. a	53. b	54. b	55. b	56. b	57. a	58. b	59. b	60. b
61. b	62. b	63. b	64. a	65. a	66. b	67. a	68. a	69. b	70. b
71. b	72. b	73. a	74. b	75. b	76. a	77. b	78. a	79. a	80. a
81. b	82. b	83. b	84. a	85. a	86. b	87. a	88. b	89. a	90. a
91. a	92. b	93. b	94. a	95. b	96. a	97. b	98. a	99. b	100. a
101. b	102. a	103. a	104. b	105. a	106. a	107. a	108. a	109. a	110. a
111. b	112. b	113. b	114. a	115. a	116. a	117. a	118. a	119. b	120. b
121. b	122. a	123. a	124. b	125. b	126. b	127. a	128. b	129. a	130. b
131. b	132. a	133. a	134. b	135. a	136. b	137. b	138. b	139. a	140. a
141. a	142. b	143. b	144. b	145. a	146. a	147. b			

Chapter 5

1. a	2. a	3. a	4. a	5. a	6. a	7. b	8. b	9. a	10. a
11. a	12. a	13. a	14. a	15. b	16. b	17. a	18. b	19. b	20. a
21. a	22. b	23. a	24. a	25. b	26. b	27. a	28. b	29. a	30. a
31. a	32. a	33. b	34. a	35. b	36. a	37. b	38. b	39. b	40. b
41. a	42. b	43. b	44. b	45. b	46. a	47. b	48. b	49. a	50. b
51. a	52. b	53. a	54. a	55. a	56. b	57. a	58. a	59. a	60. b
61. a	62. b	63. a	64. b	65. a	66. b	67. b	68. a	69. b	70. b
71. a	72. a	73. b	74. b	75. a	76. a	77. a	78. b	79. a	80. a
81. b	82. b	83. b	84. a	85. b	86. b	87. a	88. b	89. a	90. b
91. a	92. a	93. a	94. a	95. a	96. b	97. b	98. b	99. a	100. a
101. a	102. b	103. b	104. a	105. b	106. b	107. b	108. a	109. a	110. a
111. b	112. b	113. b	114. b	115. b	116. b	117. a	118. a	119. a	120. b
121. a	122. a	123. a	124. a	125. a	126. b	127. b	128. a	129. b	130. b
131. b	132. b	133. b	134. a	135. a	136. b	137. a	138. b	139. b	140. a
141. b	142. a	143. b	144. b	145. b	146. b	147. b			

Chapter 6

1. a	2. b	3. b	4. b	5. a	6. a	7. b	8. a	9. a	10. a
11. b	12. b	13. a	14. a	15. a	16. a	17. a	18. b	19. b	20. b
21. b	22. b	23. a	24. b	25. a	26. a	27. a	28. a	29. a	30. a
31. b	32. a	33. b	34. a	35. a	36. a	37. b	38. b	39. b	40. a
41. b	42. b	43. a	44. b	45. b	46. a	47. b	48. a	49. a	50. a
51. a	52. a	53. b	54. b	55. b	56. b	57. a	58. b	59. a	60. b
61. b	62. a	63. b	64. b	65. a	66. b	67. a	68. a	69. a	70. a
71. b	72. a	73. b	74. a	75. a	76. a	77. b	78. b	79. a	80. a
81. b	82. b	83. a	84. a	85. a	86. a	87. b	88. a	89. a	90. a
91. b	92. b	93. b	94. a	95. b	96. a	97. b	98. b	99. a	100. a
101. a	102. b	103. a	104. a	105. a	106. a	107. b	108. b	109. a	110. b
111. b	112. b	113. a	114. a	115. b	116. a	117. a	118. a	119. a	120. b

Chapter 7

1. b	2. b	3. a	4. b	5. b	6. a	7. b	8. b	9. a	10. b
11. b	12. b	13. a	14. a	15. b	16. b	17. b	18. a	19. a	20. a
21. a	22. a	23. b	24. a	25. a	26. b	27. b	28. b	29. b	30. a
31. a	32. b	33. a	34. b	35. a	36. a	37. b	38. b	39. b	40. a
41. a	42. a	43. b	44. b	45. a	46. b	47. a	48. b	49. a	50. a
51. b	52. a	53. a	54. a	55. a	56. a	57. a	58. b	59. a	60. a
61. a	62. b	63. b	64. b	65. a	66. a	67. b	68. b	69. b	70. a
71. b	72. b	73. a	74. b	75. b	76. b	77. a	78. b	79. b	80. a
81. a	82. a	83. a	84. a	85. a	86. b	87. a	88. b	89. a	90. a
91. b									

Chapter 8

1. b	2. b	3. b	4. b	5. b	6. a	7. b	8. a	9. b	10. b
11. a	12. a	13. a	14. b	15. a	16. b	17. a	18. b	19. b	20. a
21. a	22. b	23. a	24. b	25. a	26. a	27. b	28. b	29. b	30. a
31. b	32. a	33. a	34. b	35. a	36. b	37. b	38. b	39. b	40. a
41. b	42. b	43. a	44. b	45. b	46. a	47. a	48. a	49. b	50. b
51. b	52. a	53. a	54. a	55. b	56. a	57. a	58. a	59. b	60. b
61. b	62. b	63. b	64. a	65. a	66. a	67. a	68. a	69. b	70. b
71. a	72. b	73. a	74. b	75. a	76. a	77. a	78. b	79. a	80. a
81. b	82. b	83. a	84. a	85. a	86. b	87. b	88. a	89. b	90. b
91. b	92. a	93. a							

ANSWER KEY

Chapter 9

1. a	2. a	3. a	4. a	5. b	6. a	7. b	8. a	9. a	10. a
11. b	12. b	13. b	14. b	15. a	16. b	17. a	18. a	19. b	20. b
21. b	22. a	23. a	24. b	25. b	26. b	27. a	28. a	29. a	30. a
31. a	32. b	33. a	34. b	35. b	36. b	37. b	38. b	39. b	40. b
41. b	42. a	43. a	44. b	45. a	46. b	47. a	48. b	49. b	50. b
51. b	52. a	53. a	54. b	55. b	56. a	57. a	58. a	59. b	60. a
61. a	62. b	63. a	64. a	65. b	66. a	67. b	68. b	69. a	70. a
71. a	72. b	73. a	74. a	75. b	76. b	77. b	78. a	79. a	80. b
81. b	82. b	83. b	84. b	85. a	86. a	87. b	88. b	89. b	90. b
91. b	92. a	93. b	94. a	95. b	96. a	97. b	98. b	99. b	100. a
101. a	102. a	103. a							

Chapter 10

1. b	2. a	3. a	4. b	5. b	6. a	7. b	8. a	9. b	10. b
11. b	12. a	13. b	14. b	15. b	16. b	17. a	18. a	19. a	20. b
21. b	22. a	23. b	24. b	25. b	26. b	27. a	28. b	29. a	30. b

Chapter 11

1. a	2. b	3. b	4. b	5. b	6. a	7. a	8. a	9. b	10. a
11. b	12. b	13. b	14. a	15. b	16. a	17. a	18. a	19. b	20. b

Chapter 12

1. b	2. b	3. b	4. b	5. a	6. a	7. b	8. a	9. b	10. b
11. b	12. b	13. b	14. a	15. a	16. a	17. b	18. b	19. a	20. b
21. b	22. a	23. b	24. a	25. a	26. a	27. a	28. b	29. b	30. b
31. a	32. b	33. a	34. a	35. a	36. a	37. a	38. a	39. b	40. a
41. a	42. b	43. a	44. a	45. a	46. b	47. b	48. b	49. a	50. b
51. b	52. b	53. a	54. b	55. b	56. a	57. b	58. b	59. a	60. b
61. b	62. b	63. b	64. a	65. b	66. b	67. a	68. b	69. b	70. a
71. a	72. a	73. b	74. b	75. a	76. b	77. b	78. b	79. b	80. a
81. b	82. b	83. b	84. a	85. a	86. b	87. b	88. a	89. a	

www.ingramcontent.com/pod-product-compliance
Lightning Source LLC
Chambersburg PA
CBHW082042230426
43670CB00016B/2746